First takeoff of a Marauder. On board 40-1361 William E. "Ken" Ebel, Martin's Chief engineer and test pilot, is rotating the aircraft for its first flight on 25 November 1940. (SDAM)

Work on the most famous Martin aircraft began when the Army Air Corps asked, in January 1939, for a new high-speed medium bomber. The specification stipulated an aircraft, with a crew of five, which would be able to fly at 350 mph (563 km/h) which was faster than any operational fighter at that time, have a good range and operational ceiling. The aircraft was also required to carry 4,000 lb of bombs and have a defensive armament of four light, 0.30 inch, machine guns. With war clouds gathering over Europe and the feeling that the United States would, sooner or later, become involved no prototypes were ordered and the first aircraft off the production line was expected to be fully combat capable.

Martin began work on its Model 179, which was intended for large scale production and, from the beginning, Martin's engineers decided to incorporate as many advanced features, structural, aerodynamic, internal systems and armament, as were possible in the time available. The result was the first combat aircraft to use a four-bladed propeller, have a power-operated gun turret and incorporated the first all-plexiglas bombardier's nose position. Many new features, large and small, were incorporated as the design progressed. Its competitors were the North American NA-62 (which later became the B-25 Mitchell) and the Douglas B-23. By selecting the Martin 179 the

USAAF chose the most advanced aircraft to equip its operational medium bomb groups.

A NEW BOMBER IS BORN

The first contract, AC13243 s/n 40-1361/1561, for 201 B-26s - the designation given to Martin's aircraft - was signed on 20 September 1939, just two weeks after war broke out in Europe. The contract was for a smaller number of aircraft than the 385 originally intended as the USAAF decision makers thought that it might be prudent to split the order with the more conventional B-25 Mitchell, in case the B-26 encountered too many technical problems during its development phase. Fourteen months later, on 25 November 1940, 40-1391 the first production B-26 made its first flight. This aircraft effectively served as the prototype and this, and the second aircraft, 40-1392, which followed in February 1941 were reserved for test purposes. Trials began immediately and the first unit chosen to operate the new bomber, the 22nd BG based at Langley Field Virginia, took its first machines on charge in mid-February. Two other groups, 38th (also at Langley) and 42nd (Fort Douglas) were scheduled to be equipped with B-26s as soon as a sufficient number were available. The type had recently been christened Marauder by the British and the Americans adopted this name. Throughout 1941

A well-known photo of the B-26A 41-7347, taken in late 1941, showing the short span wings of this the third production B-26A as has the coloured cowl ring, which was used to identify the squadrons within groups. These were normally removed from all Marauders just before Pearl Harbor. *(SDAM)*

the B-26s were grounded on a number of occasions due to various technical failures, which slowed down deliveries planned for the summer of 1941. However, by Autumn of that year the main problems had been resolved and the 22nd was totally equipped with the type, while the 38th began to receive its own machines, followed by the 42nd BG, and the three Groups were fully equipped with B-26s three weeks before the attack on Pearl Harbor.

Meanwhile, on 16 September 1940, the Army ordered 139 B-26As (41-7345/7483 against contract AC13243/4). Externally identical to the B-26, the A model had additional armour plate, Goodyear rubber self-sealing fuel tanks replacing the original "Mareng" (Martin Engineering) ones and switched to a 24-volt electrical system. Provision was made for a second jettisonable 250-gallon fuel tank to be installed in the forward bomb bay as well as a low pressure oxygen system and a 100-amp generator. However all of these improvements increased the gross weight by 2,000 pounds.

The first aircraft were accepted on 31 October 1941 and by 7 April 1942 all of the B-26As had been delivered to the Army Air Force. Nevertheless, this model had a limited career with the AAF as, while the B-26As were still being delivered, the US Government agreed to release 71 of them to the British as they were the only variant immediately available which was not yet in service with AAF units. With more than half of the B-26As reserved for the RAF the AAF had less than 60 aircraft to allot to combat units, as a number of aircraft had already been lost in accidents. This was not enough to equip a single Medium Bombardment Group as the number normally allotted to a Medium Bombardment Group was 57 (thirteen per squadron plus five for Group HQ, spare not included). The B-26As could not be used either as replacement aircraft for the B-26 units already sent overseas because of the different systems installed, causing maintenance problem in the field. So no B-26A served overseas in US markings and all remained stateside to serve as trainers for other Marauder units scheduled to serve overseas. However the B-26A arrived in time to fulfil a vital role when the need for ever more Marauder crews had become crucial during Summer 1942.

The B-26As served in this role until Autumn 1943 by which time later marks of the Marauders had been built in sufficient numbers to supply the needs of overseas combat units and stateside training establishments. From that date most of the B-26As which had survived were grounded and served as instructional airframes until the end of the war.

B-26A-1 41-7462 showing the American Mk-13 torpedo carried under the belly. The "B-26A-1" denomination officially took effect on 13 April 1942. Because of a shortage of the P&W R-2800-5 equipping the type the US Air Force asked Pratt & Whitney to divert similar engines ordered by the RAF. They became R-2800-39, but the B-26A and B-26A-1 were otherwise identical. Note the censored insignia on the nose. *(SDAM)*

THE B-26A IN THE UNITED STATES

As soon as the decision was taken not to send the B-26As overseas, but use them Stateside as trainers, most served in the few specifically Marauder units.

During the war the B-26s which remained in the States were located in three major places to give operational training to the crews. At first two units were chosen to become B-26 OTUs, the 17th BG at Barksdale Field (Shreveport, LA), and the 21st BG at MacDill Field (Tampa, FL), each having an auxiliary and a training field, respectively Esler and Harding (Baton Rouge) for the 17th BG and Hillsborough-Henderson and Drane (Lakeland) for the 21st BG. The 17th BG was sent to North Africa in December 1942 and when the 21st BG was disbanded in October 1943 the aircraft were transferred to other training units.

Nevertheless in the months following Pearl Harbor additional training facilities were requi-red and new units were formed. The first was a unit to provide transitional training between the flying schools and the OTUs. The high accident rate, due to the student pilots' lack of flying experience, obliged the AAF to give additional training on the Marauder before swit-ching to the operational training syllabus. Therefore a B-26 Transition School was formed at Tarrant (Fort Worth, TX) in November 1942, and on 1 February 1943, the school moved at Laughlin (Del Rio, TX). A similar school was also opened at Dodge City, KS in April 1943.

In the meantime the USAAF formed two new units under the control of the 3rd AF. The 335th BG at Barksdale and the 336th BG at MacDill, served as RTUs (Replacement Training Unit), to supply replacement crews for units serving overseas. The 335th BG inherited most of the 17th BG's B-26As, however it seems that a few B-26As also served with the 336th BG. When those units became 331st and 332nd AAF Base Units on 1 May 1944, no B-26A were still flying with these units as they had been been replaced by newer sub-types.

The B-26As served also at other fields, as instructional airframes (or Class 26 in USAAF nomenclature), namely at Baer (IA), Bryan (TX), Buckley (CO), Keesler (MI), Lowry (CO), Scott (IL), Sheppard (TX) or Stinson (TX).

At Eglin some B-26As were sent to the 1st Minimum Altitude Bombardment and Torpedo Unit, a AAF establishment, where research and development testing was carried out.

The B-26A had a high attrition rate. Of the 68 aircraft in the USAAFs inventory 32 had been wrecked causing the death of 67 airmen.

All the B-26As which remained with the AAF in the United States were used as trainers. This one, 41-7417, is at the B-26 Transition School based at Tarrant Field (Fort Worth), Texas in 1943. By 1943, all the remaining B-26As received the prefix let-ter "R" for *Restricted* and became RB-26A, to prevent any use in operations of the type. (*USAF*)

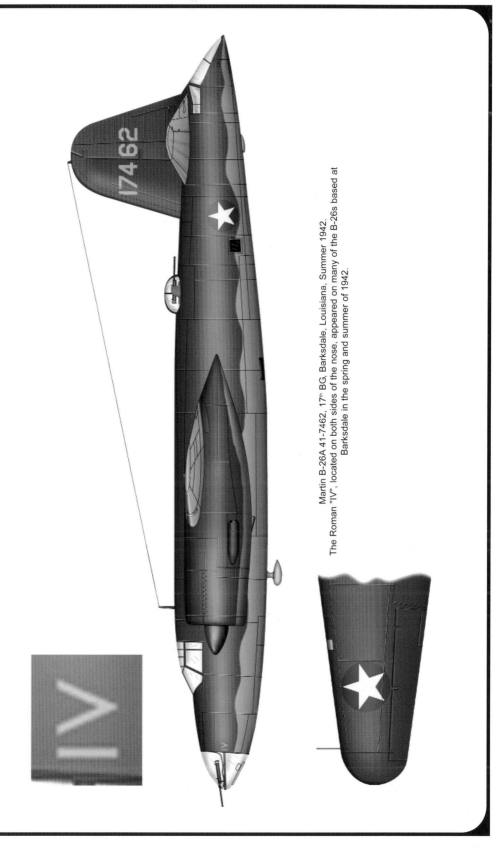

Martin B-26A 41-7462, 17th BG, Barksdale, Louisiana, Summer 1942.
The Roman "IV", located on both sides of the nose, appeared on many of the B-26s based at Barksdale in the spring and summer of 1942.

MARAUDERS FOR THE RAF

By end of 1940 the United Kingdom, and its overseas dominions, were alone in fighting against Germany. The production resources around the Commonwealth were fully occupied in producing British aircraft for the war, but there were nowhere near enough of them. The only alternative was to look for aircraft in the United States, and the British Purchasing Commission in Washington was allowed to buy almost anything it wanted. At the beginning of Autumn 1940 the RAF showed a great interest in the Marauder as a medium bomber. Indeed the RAF's strategy was to attack Germany by night, and industrial efforts were directed to producing medium and heavy bombers for this purpose. However the RAF still needed aircraft for daylight raids and, to fulfil that role, two types were in use. These were the Bristol Blenheim, which was approaching the end of its operational career, and the Douglas Boston (called the Havoc in the USA), for which a successor had also to be found.

In March 1941 the Lend-Lease agreement was approved by the American Congress and this gave a new breath of life to the Commonwealth war effort. New types were studied and an agreement was signed on 9 April 1941 for 500 aircraft to be built for the RAF under Requisition BSC-150, and these were allocated RAF serial numbers FB418-FB917. In accordance with initial Lend-Lease practice, it was intended that these aircraft would be ordered under Contract DA-46 of 26 June 1941 (with the American serials 41-31573/41-32072), and built as B-26Bs. Meanwhile the British were exerting great pressure to get the Marauder into RAF service and the AAF agreed to release 71 Marauders already in production. As previously stated the only type available was the B-26A which became the Marauder Mk.I in the RAF and the seventy-one aircraft received the serials FK109-160 (52) and FK362-380 (19).

In checking the movement cards (AMF78) it seems that no Marauder Mk.IAs actually existed, and this designation, given to the last batch of Marauders (FK362-380), seems to be unsubstantiated as all the aircraft came from the same batch of B-26As. Knowing that the Marauder Mk.IIs were similar to the B-26B-15 and later models, it is possible that this designation was reserved for the first B-26Bs with manually operated tail turrets (B-26Bs to B-26B-4s), which the RAF received in North Africa, but were never taken directly on charge. However some actually served with the RAF and SAAF (and the French as well) in North Africa from 1943 onwards, having been transferred, in the field, by the American units when new and improved models of B-26s arrived in North Africa as replacements for the Medium Bomb Groups which had suffered heavy losses during the first stages of their war in North Africa.

Before reaching North Africa the Marauder Mk.Is had to cross the Atlantic. This one, waiting at Dorval (Montreal, Quebec) in August 1942, can be seen alongside a Lockheed Ventura. It was probably one of the four Marauders which was sent to the UK in 1942 as all the others were directly sent to Africa from Miami. A dangerous task actually, as three Marauders Mk.Is never arrived to destination.

EARLY B-26Bs USED BY THE RAF

Serial	Type	US del. date	Status	SOC
41-17761	B-1-MA	26.07.42	on loan	09.11.44
41-17765	B-1-MA	26.07.42	on loan	27.07.45
41-17776	B-1-MA	02.08.42	on loan	17.08.44
41-17780*	B-1-MA	02.08.42	Tr:27.09.43	29.03.44
41-17796	B-1-MA	09.08.42	on loan	09.09.44
41-17825	B-1-MA	12.08.42	on loan	17.09.44
41-17831	B-1-MA	16.08.42	on loan	03.06.44
41-17877	B-2-MA	27.08.42	on loan	11.09.44
41-17897*	B-2-MA	04.09.42	Tr:25.09.43	01.03.46
41-17900	B-2-MA	03.09.42	on loan	27.02.44
41-17958*	B-3-MA	21.09.42	Tr:26.09.43	01.03.46
41-17977*	B-4-MA	20.10.42	Tr:25.09.43	n/a
41-17978	B-4-MA	20.10.42	Tr:26.09.43	n/a
41-18017*	B-4-MA	02.11.42	Tr:18.09.43	01.07.44
41-18031	B-4-MA	06.11.42	Tr:18.09.43	n/a
41-18037*	B-4-MA	05.11.42	Tr:18.09.43	n/a
41-18039*	B-4-MA	06.11.42	Tr:31.08.43	26.08.44
41-18041	B-4-MA	06.11.42	Tr:31.08.43	n/a
41-18046	B-4-MA	10.11.42	on loan	17.09.44
41-18197	B-10-MA	20.01.43	on loan	17.09.43

*Known to have been used in operations. The other were used for training. [Tr : Theatre transfer].

The new tail turret introduced on the B-26B. Similar B-26Bs used by the RAF had been transferred in the field from the Americans. Some were even used operationally by No.14 Squadron after a shortage of Marauder Mk.Is but most were used as training aircraft. Except for the tail turret those B-26Bs were very similar to the B-26As. They were sometimes referred to as Marauder Mk.IAs in No.14 Squadron's documents, but this denomination remained unofficial. (USAF)

TECHNICAL DATA
B-26A/MARAUDER MK.I

Manufacturer and production:
139 by Martin (Baltimore)

Type :
land-based medium bomber.

Accomodation (RAF) :
Six : Pilot, Second Pilot, Air Bomber/nose gunner, Navigator, Wireless Operator/Gunner (turret), Air Gunner (tail).

Power plants :
Two Pratt & Whitney Double Wasp R-2800-5 eighteen-cylinder (two rows) radial air-cooled rated 1,850 hp **[B-26A]** or R-2800-39 rated 2,000 hp **[B-26A-1]**

Fuel & Oil
Fuel (US Gal):
Normal capacity : 962 [3 633 l] &
two 250 gallons [944 l] extra tanks in the bomb bay.

Oil (US Gal):
Standard per engine : 41.25 [156 l]

Dimensions :
Span : 65 ft 0-in [19,81 m]
Length : 56 ft 0-in [17,05 m]
Height : 19 ft 10-in [6,04 m]
Wing area : 602 Sq ft [183,49 m²]

Weights :
Empty : 21,741 lb [9 861 kg]
Gross : 28,376 lb [12 871 kg]

Performance :
Max speed :
315 mph at 15,000 ft
[507 km/h à 4 500 m]

Cruising speed : 258 mph [415 km/h]

Service ceiling : 25,000 ft [7 600 m]

Normal range : 1,000 miles [1 600 km]

Endurance at range speed :
4h00 (with internal fuel)
over 10h00
(with extra bomb bay tanks fuel and no military load)

Armament :
1 x 0.30-in [7.62 mm] in the nose with 500 rounds.
2 x 0.50-in [12.7mm] in dorsal turret with 400 rpg.
1 x 0.50-in [12.7mm] in tail turret with 240 rounds.

provision for :
3,000 lb [1 361 kg] of bombs in the bobm bay
or
up to 2,000 lb [907 kg] torpedo under the belly

DELIVERIES AND STRENGHT

Month (at last day)	Transferred	Total transferred	Op. Losses	Accident	SOC	On Hand
February 42	52	52	-	-	-	52
March 42	17	69	-	-	-	69
.../...						
July 42	-	69	-	3	1	65
August 42	-	69	-	2	-	63
September 42	-	69	-	-	-	63
October 42	-	69	-	1	-	62
November 42	-	69	-	-	1	61
December 42	-	69	2	-	-	59
January 43	-	69	1	-	-	58
February 43	-	69	4	1	-	53
March 43	-	69	-	2	-	51
April 43	-	69	2	-	-	49
May 43	-	69	2	1	-	46
June 43	-	69	2	2	-	42
July 43	-	69	1	3	-	38
August 43	-	69	1	-	-	37
September 43	-	69	1	-	-	36
October 43	-	69	1	1	-	34
November 43	-	69	-	-	-	34
December 43	-	69	1	2	-	31
January 44	-	69	-	-	-	31
February 44	-	69	1	3	-	27
March 44	-	69	-	-	-	27
April 44	-	69	1	2	-	24
May 44	-	69	2	-	-	22
.../...						
September 44	-	69	3	1	-	18
October 44	-	69	-	-	-	18
November 44	-	69	-	-	1	17
.../...						
March 45	-	69	-	-	3	14
April 45	-	69	-	-	1	13
.../...						
July 45	-	69	-	-	7	6 [1]

[1] The remaining aircraft were officially struck off charge on 1 January 1947, but they were probably scrapped well before that date.

Marauder FK138 was one of the four aircraft of that type which were sent to the United Kingdom for testing. They were retained for this purpose until Spring 1944 when they were ferried to the Middle East where they were delivered to No.14 Squadron, which was experiencing a high attrition rate. Sadly it became the last loss sustained by No.14 Squadron. *(IWM CH17449)*

Marauder FK111 was the first to arrive in the United Kingdom and, like all the new types coming into service with the RAF, a set of photographs were taken to be published in recognition manuals and other publications. (*Phil Jarrett*)

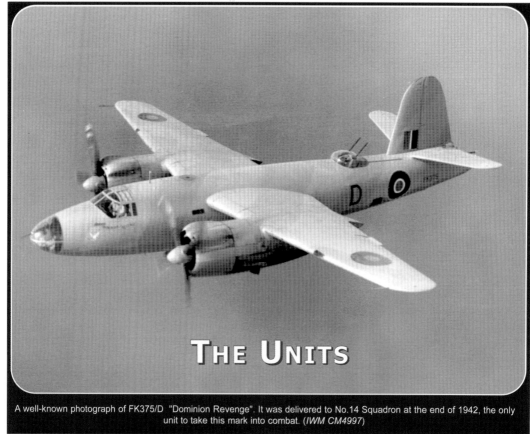

THE UNITS

A well-known photograph of FK375/D "Dominion Revenge". It was delivered to No.14 Squadron at the end of 1942, the only unit to take this mark into combat. (*IWM CM4997*)

No.14 Squadron
August 1942 - September 1944

With so few Marauders available, the RAF could not put this mark into large scale service. As the Mitchell was also being delivered at this time, and scheduled to be used from English airfields to support Boston operations, the Marauders were sent directly from the United States to the Middle East where reinforcements were most needed. As they could carry a torpedo this was an additional reason for sending the type to the Mediterranean Theatre. The Italian merchant fleet, which was supplying Axis forces in North Africa, had to be hunted down and destroyed as quickly as possible.

The unit selected to operate the Marauder Mk.I was No.14 Squadron, a bomber unit, which had been at war since September 1939 and had previously flown Wellesleys and Blenheims, and became the only operational unit user of this mark. Based in Egypt since November 1941 it had carried out day and night raids and the Squadron needed to be rested so it was seen as a good can-

didate to be retrained on the Marauder. For this reason the squadron was withdrawn from service at LG.224 Fayid, in Egypt, on 10 August 1942 for conversion to the new type.

The Squadron was commanded by Wing Commander Wynne S.G. "Dick" Maydwell and a group of USAAF personnel, led by Colonel Flint Garrison who had served with the 17th Bomb Group, were attached to the Squadron to instruct pilots and ground staff in the use of the new aircraft. In the Middle East, as in the States, the Marauder proved to be a "hot" aircraft to fly, especially while being landed, as its short wing span forced a high landing speed on pilots who had until recently flown the more tolerant aircraft of the previous generation. Against this must be balanced the experience of the British pilots. Even if they did not have the accident rate the Americans experienced with the Marauder, sometimes nicknamed the "Widow maker", it was not a forgiving aircraft at low speed and pilots had to keep this in mind to avoid finding themselves in a dangerous situation. The Americans had suffered a higher accident rate in 1941-1942 as many of their pilots had only recently graduated and had little experience of flying at low speeds and, as a result, they were not always able to master an aircraft like the Marauder. By 1944, however, with extensive experience of the aircraft, and more time to train the pilots, this accident rate become more reasonable.

In any case No.14 Squadron's crews were not able to complete their training without incident and on 20 August 1942, while returning from a familiarisation flight, Colonel Garrison crashed while landing Marauder FK157. Four Egyptians, in a truck, decided to cross the runway directly in front of the Marauder and Colonel Garrison could do nothing to avoid collision. He hit the truck killing three of the four Egyptians while the fourth was badly injured. Everybody in the aeroplane escaped injuries, however the Marauder had to be scrapped.

MARAUDER'S DEBUT

On 28 October 1942 Lieutenant Young (SAAF) and his crew took off from Fayid at 0522 hours on the first Marauder operation, a meteorological reconnaissance flight carried out by FK121/Y. The Marauder returned after having completed a flight of nearly 8 hours over the sea without incident. On 1 November it was the turn of Australian Flying Officer Elliot (FK112/L) to take off on an unarmed reconnaissance and, after 8 hours and 45 minutes, the Marauder returned to No.14 Squadron's new base at Fayid near the Suez Canal. After another single aircraft sortie, on the 2nd, the Squadron sent three Marauders, for the first time, on an operation. The first use of weapons in combat occurred on the 6th when a member of the CO's crew on FK375/D fired on a target. Flying low to avoid enemy radar they soon arrived north of Crete where they found a number of barges heading for the island. Wing Commander "Dick" Maydwell flew over them and the rear gunner, Sergeant Gil Graham, opened fire, provoking panic, and leaving the German troops with no choice but to dive overboard. The flight continued and W.S.G. Maydwell spotted an enemy troopship of 2,500 tons which was escorted by a German seaplane (identified as He115 which seems unlikely and was more probably an Ar196), and a naval sloop. The Marauder crew did not have time to react before being repeatedly hit by *flak* which wounded the turret gunner in the leg but the flight was not yet over. Shortly afterwards the Marauder came across

Wing Commander Wynne S.G. Maydwell was a pre-war RAF pilot, who served with No.53 Squadron in UK during the first years of the war, and was awarded the DFC in November 1940. He took command of No.14 Squadron in May 1942 and successfully supervised the unit's conversion to Marauders. His leadership ensured that the squadron would become a particularly effective unit. He was awarded a well earned DSO, on 9 April 1943, for his leadership and left the squadron in August 1943. He ended the war as a Group Captain having subsequently served in a number of non-operational postings.
(14 Squadron Association)

another shipping convoy escorted by two destroyers and seven Ju88s. Combat could not be avoided when three of the latter altered course towards the Marauder and put the dorsal turret out of action Wing Commander Maydwell thought it unwise to accept the challenge and made good use of the Marauder's top speed to evade the Ju88s. The Germans did not follow as they had fulfilled their mission in protecting the convoy. FK375/D returned to base after eight hours flying and the gunner was taken to hospital. Meanwhile the squadron was sending out aircraft every day while training continued. The Squadron suffered its first casualties on 23

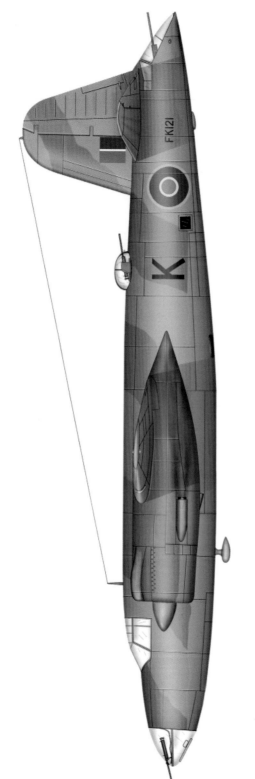

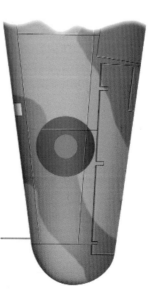

Martin Marauder Mk.I FK121, No.14 Squadron, Fayid, Egypt, Autumn 1942.

November 1942, when FK122, captained by Canadian Flying Officer William R. Bower, crashed on on the bombing range at Shallufa after the tailplane broke away, giving the crew of five no chance of surviving. At the time this weakness was one of the Marauder's main problems however this was solved a few months later.

In December, after some serious consideration, the RAF decided not to use the Marauder as a conventional medium bomber but only as torpedo-armed reconnaissance aircraft, so a part of the Squadron moved to Shaluffa to be trained in torpedo dropping. Meanwhile single aircraft reconnaissance flights were carried out over the Mediterranean where the endurance of the

from Malta which were escorting five Beaufighters on a reconnaissance mission off the Tunisian coast. The Marauder was still new to many Allied pilots and the fighters decided to close in on the formation of bombers. The Marauder's gunners seem to have been over cautious and fired at the Spitfires of No.249 Squadron led by Squadron Leader Woods. One of the Spitfire pilots, Flight Lieutenant Seed, returned fire at one of the Marauders (FK367/J), but stopped when it fired the identification colours of the day. But it was too late for the bomber which had to ditch with the loss of four of the crew. No.14 Squadron's gunners had also been accurate as Flight Lieutenant Seed's Spitfire

A formation of three Marauder Mk.Is of No.14 Squadron at the end of 1942. During its career the Marauder Mk.Ia was mainly used for over sea patrols which were usually carried out by a single aircraft and the type was rarely used in any numbers on a single operation. (*IWM CM5000*)

Marauder, with flight times regularly exceeding 7 hours, was used to its maximum. However the Marauders were sometimes used in group operations. On 16 December 1942, three aircraft, FK371/A with Flight Lieutenant D.R.W. Brown and crew, FK126/C with Flying Officer B.S. Slade and crew and FK367/J with Sergeant L.A. Einsaar and crew) were sent on an offensive sweep along the Tripolitanian Coast. No shipping was seen but as the formation set course for home the Marauders were intercepted by RAF fighters

was damaged, by Sergeant Carr in Brown's crew, and he crash-landed on his return to Malta. For his bravery during this, and for other previous actions, Sergeant Eisnaar (RAAF) was awarded a well deserved **DFM**, the first award to a Marauder crewman. A few days later, on 20 December 1942, Sergeant G.C. Egebjerg, a Dane serving in the RAF, and crew took off on board FK131/E for an offensive shipping sweep along the Tunisian coast. The Marauder was soon attacked by twin-engined German aircraft and one of the attac-

Another photo of FK375/D "Dominion Revenge" with a torpedo fixed under its belly at Gambut. The RAF used its own torpedo rack to enable it to carry the Royal Navy 18-inch torpedo instead of the American types. (*14 Squadron Association*)

kers, identified as a Bf110, was shot down by Sergeant Taylor, the tail gunner, who was injured by German bullets. It was the first "kill" claimed by a Marauder and proved that, thanks to the American 0.50-in machine gun, the best machine gun of its type at that time, it was capable of defending itself. Even so it did not prevent the loss of FK366/S, captained by Pilot Officer J.T. Willis **DFM**, and its crew which did not return from a mine-lying operation over the entrance to Tunis harbour. Five Marauders were sent out that night and, while dropping its mines, the aircraft was hit by *flak* and exploded in the air killing all on board but Willis who wa taken prisoner. John T. Willis had been a long serving member of the Squadron and had been awarded the **DFM** the previous September. The Squadron thought that they had lost another Marauder during the same mission but FK133/R, captained by C.J. O'Connor (RAAF), had landed in Malta, following fuel problems, caused by his navigator who accidentally had dropped the fuel tank in the bomb bay with the mines! The crew returned to base the following day.

SLOW BEGINNINGS

At the end of 1942, and the beginning of 1943, No.14 Squadron was facing various logistical problems which reduced its rate of combat sorties. This was partially due to training requirements causing a shortage of aircraft. In addition other aircraft were at various Maintenance Units waiting to be repainted and fully equipped for RAF

service. Furthermore, as the aircraft was a new type in RAF service, spares were not always available. This lack of spares was due to the small number of aircraft taken on charge by the RAF and also because the American supplied their own units first. This situation lasted until the spring of 1943. On average only one Marauder was available for operation each day during January and February 1943. However this low rate of sorties did not prevent additional losses. On 3 January 1943, four torpedo armed Marauders took off from Shaluffa to patrol the Aegean Sea, operating in two pairs. During this flight the pair led by South African Captain B.W. Young (FK375/D) sighted a convoy of five ships off Aghios Girogios Island, and the Marauders attacked the convoy. The other Marauder, captained by Lieutenant L.C. Jones (FK120/X), another South African, released its torpedo, the first used in an attack, but the results could not be observed. Captain B.W. Young did not drop his torpedo, and lost contact with the other Marauder. Lieutenant Jones returned to base but Captain B.W. Young's crew was posted missing. It was later established that Young's Marauder had been attacked by the escorting Bf110s which had shot it down. Captain Young was the only survivor and became a PoW. On 17 January 1943, a Ju52 was severely damaged by two Marauders during a reconnaissance flight over the Aegean Sea and it was shared between Australian Flight Sergeant O.A. Philipps' crew (FK159/W) and that of Lieutenant L.C. Jones (FK120/X). The main

event of the month occurred three days later when Pilot Officer J.H. Elliott (RAAF) and crew (FK142/Y) torpedoed, and sank, an 800 ton vessel off Melos. The escorting Ar196 could not prevent the loss of the ship. The rest of the month was generally uneventful, but on the last day of January, whilst on a training flight, Flying Officer L. Johnson (RAAF) and crew and Flying Officer D. Grimsey's crew attacked another ship off Melos, but without result. This time the escort was more efficient and Grimsey's Marauder was attacked several times by the three escorting Ju88s. In attacks which lasted for 15 minutes they claimed one German aircraft damaged and the Marauders returned to base undamaged.

February was initially quite uneventful, but on 15th the Squadron lost two aircraft during a torpedo reconnaissance over the Aegean Sea. Both aircraft took off at 1045 hours, but it was not until 16.00 hours that two wireless messages were received from FK143 (Lieutenant L.C. Jones). The first stated that the Marauder was flying on one engine and losing height, and the second that the aircraft was making a landing in neutral Turkish territory. The crew was interned but later released. The fate of FK150, the aircraft flown by Flight Sergeant C.C. Truman (RAAF), remained unknown and the crew was posted missing.

One week later the Squadron mounted its biggest operation yet when nine Marauders targeted the harbour and installation on Melos. Pilot Officer Clarke-Hall torpedoed a 5,000 ton vessel which blew up and sank. Another ship, of 4,000

tons, was sunk and this was shared by the crew of Major E.M. Lewis, SAAF (FK370/Z) and Flying Officer R.W. Lapthorne, RAAF (FK151/O). A third ship was attacked by Flying Officer O.A. Philipps, RAAF and Flying Officer E. Donovan but the results were unobserved. Meanwhile the other Marauders bombed land based targets and claimed direct hits on various buildings. Once again this task proved dangerous and, for the second time in the month, the Squadron lost two Marauders on the same day when the aircraft flown by Sergeant R.A. Barton (RAAF), FK377 and Sergeant B.H. Yarwood FK139/M did not return from the raid. No more operational sorties were carried out until the end of the month. But with such heavy losses sustained in this kind of operations, no torpedo-bombing operations was to be planned anymore and No.14 Squadron ceased to be a torpedo-bomber squadron and became a conventional Coastal Command reconnaissance unit.

MOVING WESTWARD

With the liberation of North Africa under way the Squadron moved westwards to be closer to the front line. On the first day of March part of the Squadron moved to Telergma in North Africa, a USAAF controlled base, while the remaining personnel and aircraft stayed at Shallufa, under the command of Flying Officer R.W. Lapthorne (RAAF), and the overall authority of No.5 M.E.T.S. Here it continued to train aircrew and to supply replacement aircraft and fully operational trained aircrew as required. Detachments also

An unidentified Marauder Mk.I being serviced at Gambut 3 at the beginning of 1943. (*via Peter H.T. Green*)

Most of the Marauder Mk.I were used with the American Olive Drab/Light Grey like FK124/Z, seen here on detachment to Gambut 3. (*F.M. Spedding via Paul Sortehaug*)

remained at Berka and Gambut. After a short stay at Telergma the Squadron moved to Blida where it stayed for the next three months. An advanced flight of two Marauders took off on 10 March 1943 but the weather encountered was not as forecast, and one the aircraft, FK154/K, piloted by Squadron Leader P. Goode crashed into the Bay of Algiers causing the death of the eight men on board. This included the Squadron Intelligence Officer (H.M. Siewart) and two ground-crew. The remaining 14 Marauders arrived at Berka on the 12th without incident.

Back in Egypt however another accident occurred on the 18th when FK117 crashed whilst practising circuits on one engine. The two pilots were severely injured in the crash but survived while LAC J.I. Lewis, who was serving as the Flight Engineer, was killed. It seems that the pilots were not able to re-start the second engine and tried to land on one, something which was particularly difficult to do in a short winged Marauder. At Blida operational sorties resumed on 22 March 1943 and the rest of the month was uneventful. In April it was decided to create a training flight within the unit and No.14 Squadron, which was the only user of the Marauder Mk.I, had to provide its own replacement aircrew. To distinguish the aircraft of the training flight from the operational Marauders a "T" was added to the letter identifying the aircraft. Over 90 sorties and 600 operational flying hours were performed during

the month and, six months after the introduction of the type, the Squadron was now fully operational and mounted sorties almost every day in April. With such a high sortie rate its contribution to the campaign was significant and, on 8 April 1943, the Squadron received a congratulatory message from HQ Mediterranean Allied Coastal Air Forces (MACAF) for one its reconnaissance sorties which resulted in the complete destruction of an enemy convoy. But a price had to be paid for this success and on 12 April 1943, FK378/G, flown by Warrant Officer L.A. Eisnaar (RAAF) was posted missing, shot down by FW190s, while on a reconnaissance flight. All the crew but one survived to become PoWs. Enemy fighters were always dangerous and four days later FK160/H (Flight Sergeant F.W.T. Bates and crew) was attacked by two Me210s and returned to base with bullet holes in the fuselage. Encounters with the Luftwaffe happened almost every day and one He115, one Ju88, one Cant Z.501 and one He59 were claimed as damaged in the same period. On 24 April FK364/B crashed on return and all but two of the crew were injured and had to be admitted to hospital. However Flight Sergeant Bedell died of wounds soon afterwards. The following day another Marauder, FK371/A, was lost and the crew was posted missing. The last day of the month could have ended with another tragedy when four American Lightnings attacked FK144/M but stopped their

attack when they saw the colours of the day being fired by the Marauder crew.

In May the Squadron continued to screen the Mediterranean Sea from the Tunisian coast and the squadron's aircraft were based at Blida, Bone and Bizerte. However losses continued and on the 9th FK155/V was posted missing. Flight Sergeant T.G.N. Russell, RAAF had taken off at 0530 hours from Bone but nothing was heard after that. They probably encountered enemy fighters which were very active in the area, as Flying Officer C.P.M. Philipps (FK373/S) could testify when he was chased by two FW190s for fifteen minutes on the 13th. Fortunately he escaped undamaged. Sometimes less dangerous aircraft were sighted and attacked as on the 15th when Sergeant H.E. Rawlins (from Kenya) and the crew of FK145/N claimed a Ju52

THE MARAUDER : A DEADLY WEAPON!

On 3 June 1943 No.14 Squadron recorded another loss when Sergeant H.E. Rawlins and crew in FK112/E failed to return. He took off at 0858 hours and sighted a convoy at 1306 hours. Nothing was heard after that and it is believed that he was shot down by the convoy's escort. But Rawlins' crew was revenged the following week when, on 10 June 1943, Flight Sergeant Bates and crew, FK144/M, shot down an Italian SM82 (or more probably a SM79) on the return flight to Blida. The Italians tried to escape by diving towards the sea to gain speed but the Marauder had a clear speed advantage and closed on the port side of the SM82. The Marauder's turret gunner was easily able to follow the Italian aircraft and with a few well placed shots sent the

An unidentified aircraft taken during its ferry flight from a maintenance unit to No.14 Squadron, during the spring of 1943. All the machine guns have been installed but the Marauder has not yet had its individual letter applied to the fuselage.
(ww2.images.com)

as damaged. Two days later Flight Lieutenant F.H. Brown (FK147/B) attacked a Me323 without success and later Flight Sergeant H.W.T. Bates (FK120/X) sighted six Me323s but had to abandon the attack when their guns jammed. On 22 May 1943 Me323s were again encountered and this time luck was with No.14 Squadron. Squadron Leader H. Law-Wright (FK160/H) attacked a formation of three of these very large aircraft and shot the No.3 aircraft down into sea. He then attacked the leader of the formation but when he was in position to shoot it down his guns jammed.

Italians into sea. Later that day Flying Officer M.C. Johnson (FK123/J) was attacked by eight Bf109s escorting a float plane. The Bf109s attacked with confidence thinking that it was an easy target just waiting to be shot down but the tail gunner, Flight Sergeant G.D. Gilbert fired first and brought the German pilots back to reality by shooting down one of the attackers. A few seconds later he destroyed a second one while a third Bf109 was seen trailing black smoke as it hastily departed. The remaining Germans decided to break off the action, which was a good decision for the Marauder's gunners who were running out of ammunition. On the 11th Flying Officer E. Donovan (FK147/B) sighted a convoy but could not get too close because of accurate anti-aircraft fire. Later he crossed paths with two Bf109s which attacked the Marauder. The 109s fired but missed their target and as one of the fighters turned to port it gave the turret gunner the opportunity to bring his guns to bear and fire. The 109 went over on its back and dived into the sea. The other Bf109 again attacked but was hit by both turret and tail gunners. It then gave up and was last seen losing height but no claim was made. The following day it was the turn of Lieutenant G.K. Graham, SAAF to claim a Ju52 as damaged. That same day, Major E. Lewis, the A Flight leader, left the Squadron having completed his tour of operations. He was one of the most experienced pilots in the Squadron at that time. Before the end of the month Flying Officer M.C. Johnson's crew, in FK159/W, claimed a Me210, but the Squadron sustained another loss when FK363/G failed to return from an operation.

During the first week of July the squadron lost two Marauders in accidents. The first, FK141, on the 8th while being ferried from the Middle East, with three fatalities, and on the 10th when Flying Officer C.F.M. Philipps crash-landed FK152 resulting in the deaths of five crew members including himself. Three days later Flying Officer Parker, and his crew, completed their tour of 250 hours, a first for a Marauder crew.

On 15 July 1943 Wing Commander Maydwell and his crew in FK147/B claimed the destruction of a SM 82. Once again the Marauder proved to be a deadly opponent. Unfortunately the same aircraft was lost just two weeks later, on the 24th, during a shipping reconnaissance in the Elba-Corsica-Spezia area. Following an attack by two FW190s Flight Sergeant J.D. Hunter (RAAF) ditched the Marauder and all the crew members were picked up and became PoWs. On 22 July, Wing Commander Maydwell (FK149/D) was again lucky and came across a Ju90 heading towards Bastia aerodrome in Corsica. The gunners fired 180 rounds from 150 yards, the port inner engine was seen to stop, oil poured from it and was it claimed as damaged (in fact the Ju 90 crashed soon afterwards). The month ended with the CO and his crew, flying FK142/R, shooting down a Me323 which crashed into the base of a hill near Cape Corse. Some photographs were taken during this action and these later appeared in a Tunis newspaper which gave the Marauder, and No.14 Squadron, some very good publicity. The CO was not the only one to distinguished himself as, shortly afterwards Flying Officer H. Elsey and crew (FK156/O) attacked a formation of nine Ju52s damaging three of them without themselves sustaining any damage.

22 July 1943. An impressive photo showing the attack on a Ju 90 by Wing Commander Maydwell's crew. The badly damaged four-engined German aircraft crashed a few seconds later near Bastia aerodrome (Corsica) while trying to make an emergency landing. (*14 Squadron Association*)

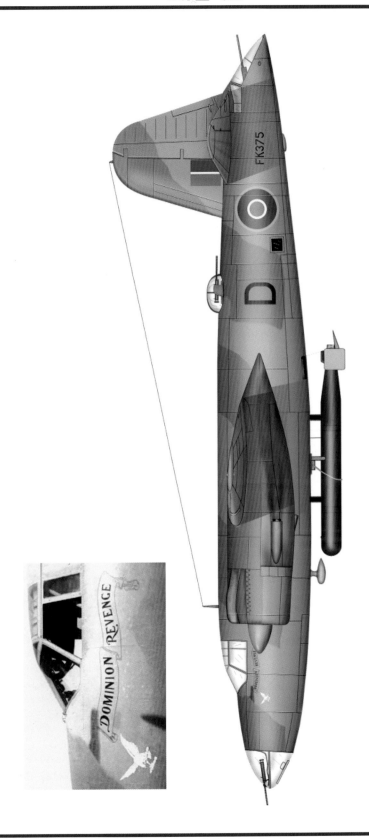

Martin Marauder Mk.I FK375, "Dominion Revenge" No.14 Squadron, Gambut, Libya, January 1943.
The torpedo is a Royal Navy 18-in type.
The small patch on the nose is actually the original Olive Drab paint where the USAAF serial was located.

One of a number of impressive photographs taken on 24 July 1943 which shows Wing Commander Maydwell attacking a Me 323. Some of those photos were later published in a Tunis newspaper. (*14 Squadron Association*)

On 5 August 1943 it was the turn of Squadron Leader H. Law-Wright and crew (FK362/H) to make hits on German aircraft, the victims being two He111s. During a reconnaissance flight the crew sighted two vics of 3 He111s and Squadron Leader Law-Wright attacked immediately. Closing to within 40 feet of the German aircraft hits were observed, by the tail gunner, on the nose of No.2 of the second vic and the leader of the same vic was set on fire. The Heinkels returned fire without any success. Other encounters took place over the following two days. On the 6th Flying Officer E. Donovan was chased for ten minutes by five FW190s based in Corsica. The gunners of Marauder FK121/Y got hits on two of the attackers and smoke was seen coming from their engines. The following day it was the turn of Flying Officer C.R. Thomson's crew (FK145/N) to be attacked, this time by two Bf109s. The turret gunner's shooting was accurate, hitting one Bf109 on its first attack and obliging the pilot to break off. This 109 disappeared from the action with smoke and fumes trailing from its engine whilst the second carried out four attacks before it too was hit and disappeared. On the 15 August, almost one year after the arrival of the Marauders, the Squadron had accumulated more than 8,100 flying hours of which half had been logged on operations. On 19 August 1943 Wing Commander Maydwell was posted to take command of C.A.F. Station, Bo Rizzo, and relinquished command to Squadron Leader H. Law-Wright who was appointed to the rank of Acting

Wing Commander. The squadron also received notification of the award of the DSO to Major E.M. Lewis, a former member of the Squadron. By the end of the month other changes occurred when command of the flights were taken over by H.S Grimsey and E. Donovan, both as Acting Squadron Leaders. But it was not all good news for the Squadron as the newly promoted Flight

On 20 August 1943 Major Eric M. Lewis, SAAF, became the second Marauder pilot to be awarded the DSO. He is one of the 35 members of the SAAF to have been appointed to this order during WW2. He spent more than two years with No.14 Squadron, flying Blenheims and Marauders, before completing his tour. He was also awarded a DFC on 7 April 1942. In November 1944 he was posted to No.16 Squadron, SAAF, which was flying Beaufighters, for another tour, becoming its CO in December until the end of war. (*14 Squadron Association*)

Wing Commander W.S.G. Maydwell posing proudly in front of FK142/R "Dominion Triumph" in which, with his crew, he shot down a Me323 on 24 July 1943. Note the evidence of the return fire from the German gunners. (*14 Squadron association*)

Lieutenant E.L. Archer (FK373/S) did not return from a reconnaissance flight on the 26th. He became a PoW, as did four other crew members, however Sergeant A. Phethean was killed. Incontestably the Marauder Mk.I and No.14 Squadron crews saw a lot of action, and were successful in action against Luftwaffe aircraft, during the summer of 1943. It would seem that the RAF had proven, before the USAAF, that the Marauder was a very good weapon in the hands of experienced aircrew.

LACK OF AIRCRAFT IN SIGHT

September was also a busy month with almost 100 sorties carried out, including seven on the 8th, following the capitulation of Italy. The Squadron tried to locate the Italian fleet, which had sailed to surrender to the Allies, but was not able to do so that day. The following day, however, Flight Lieutenant Philipps was the first to sight the fleet and shadowed it until he was relieved by Flight Sergeant Freeman (RNZAF), who was in turn relieved by the CO. The latter was patrolling close to the Italians when the battleship Roma was sunk by the Luftwaffe, but he could do nothing to prevent the tragedy. During this flight Wing Commander H. Law-Wright broke the squadron's endurance record after being airborne during 10.5 hours. Over the days which followed many encounters with enemy aircraft took place but it was not until the 18th that further claims were recorded. On this day the turret gunner of

the FK149/D (piloted by Flying Officer M. Wilsby) fired a short burst of 25 rounds at a Ju88 which struck the German aircraft, and the following day was action packed when FK142/R (Warrant Officer C.A Long and crew) was chased by six Ju88s for seven minutes, but the Marauder escaped. FK149/D (Flight Sergeant Spedding, RNZAF) were attacked by three Re2001s which damaged the Marauder's port wing. However return fire from the bomber was accurate and flames were seen coming from one of the attackers. Two days later, while on a reconnaissance sortie, FK110/E (Flying Officer D.F. Thomas) spotted seven Ju52s escorted by two Ju88s. The Ju88s tried to defend the vulnerable transport aircraft from attack by the Marauder, but it evaded the Ju88s and attacked, and the turret and tail gunners damaged two Ju52s. The Ju88s returned and these, and the heavy return fire from the Ju52s, forced the Marauder to give up the attack. On the 23rd more than 50 transport aircraft were sighted, and while some of them were attacked no results were achieved. On 27 September 1943 the squadron nearly lost another aircraft when Flight Sergeant Spedding, RNZAF, (FK128/B) was attacked by two Ar196s. Both of the Marauder's gunners opened fire at 600 yards scoring strikes on the attackers which soon broke the attack with dark fumes coming from the engine on one of the Arados. It was claimed as probable. Nevertheless a further danger awaited the Marauder and three minutes later two Bf109s were seen approaching. Accurate

Blida Spring 1943. A Marauder taxiing rapidly to the take off point prior to undertaking another patrol. (*ww2.images.com*)

fire from the tail gunner damaged one of the Bf109s and it broke away. This fact did not discourage the second Bf109's pilot who continued to attack but the Marauder evaded it on each occasion and after a few exchanges of fire the 109 withdrew without apparent damage to either aircraft. Unknown to the Marauder crew its undercarriage had been hit during the fighting and the wheels could not be lowered. It had to crash-land on the base, and while the Marauder was a total write-off none of the crew were injured.

The number of sorties remained high in October despite heavy rains. The previous month the squadron had begun to take on charge a number of war-weary early model B-26Bs from the USAAF, for training purposes, as the number of Marauders had decreased so dramatically over the year the Marauder I had been in service and were now in short supply. The idea was to reserve, as far as possible, the Marauder Is, for the operations and leave the B-26Bs for the training flights but this was not strictly adhered to. Otherwise the month was quite uneventful as enemy activity in the area had begun to decrease. On the 14th one of the ships sighted by Flight Sergeant Bates' crew was later sunk by a destroyer and a tanker captured. Co-operation with the Navy proved to be efficient in many ways as the success was repeated on the 17th when another merchant ship was captured. Unfortunately two days later the crew of FK127/K was posted missing, one crew member surviving the crash and later picked-up, who said that the loss was caused by an aileron failure. On the 24th another Marauder (FK362/H) flown by Flight

Sergeant H.E Bates was grounded, after battle damage, following an encounter with three Bf109s which had attacked from astern. The tail gunner fired all his ammunition, while the turret gunner could only manage to fire 50 rounds. The port engine and starboard propellor was damaged, but no claim could be made by the Marauder crew. Three days later the squadron moved to Sidi Amor in Tunisia.

In November the number of sorties again began to decrease and while there were many sightings nothing of importance was reported. On the 4th Flying Officer W.R. Gellatly, RNZAF, and crew (FK126/P) recorded the last claim of the year when his gunners damaged a Bf109 during a reconnaissance sortie over the southern Adriatic. On 12 November 1943, six weeks after he had been awarded the DFC, Squadron Leader H. Law-Wright was awarded the DSO, the third for the year and for a Marauder pilot. It was a well deserved award after a year of intense activity and heavy losses.

Meanwhile some problems were becoming crucial. Over the last couple of weeks No.14 Squadron had been faced with a serious shortage of Marauder Mk.Is. With an operational requirement for two flights and a training flight, and taking into account the normal number of aircraft grounded due to battle damage, maintenance or inspection, the number of Marauder Mk.Is was not nearly sufficient to meet these requirements and some of the recently supplied B-26Bs, the least war-weary ones, had to be brought up to operational standard, and included in the Squadron's inventory.

Like the Marauder Mk.I those early B-26Bs were able to carry a torpedo and one of these aircraft had its first RAF operational sortie on 26 December 1943. They continued to fly alongside the Marauder Mk.Is until the Squadron converted to Wellingtons in the autumn of 1944. Despite the arrival of the B-26Bs the Marauder Mk.I remained the crews' the first choice, because it was faster than later model, and speed was of the essance when being chased by fighters. In spite of this Marauder Is were the only subtype lost before the end of the year. FK133/A was posted missing with the loss of the full crew on 28 December 1943, while on a sortie over the Levant. With this loss, the third in the month, only 31 Marauders of the 69 taken on charge by the RAF were still available to the Squadron. This gives a clear indication of how costly the war had been in terms of men and aircraft and how intensively the Marauder Mk.I had been used during the previous 16 months.

THE LAST YEAR AND PHASING OUT

Sorties continued to be carried out in January 1944 but were uneventful, however February began with a loss of another Marauder and crew (FK142/R) on the 1st. It took off at 0920 hours for a reconnaissance around Cape Corse and was never seen again. Two days later FK126 was destroyed in an accident, fortunately without any injuries to the crew. The same day, Squadron Leader Grimsey was posted out to become the Commanding Officer of No.52 Squadron, and was replaced by Canadian Flight Lieutenant Elsey

as commander of the detachment in Italy, which was reduced to six aircraft. A couple of days later February began shaping up as the worst month for some time when, on the 8th, FK362/H was posted missing with its crew, while returning to Blida from Grottaglie. On board this Marauder was Flight Sergeant Climpson who was returning to Blida as his tour had expired. Two more Marauders, including one B-26B, were lost later in the month. B-26B (117958/B) was lost on the 17th but the crew sustained no injuries and this was followed on the 23rd by FK130/F which crashed near Grottaglie during an air test. The purpose of the flight had been to obtain cine film footage for No.2 Film Production Unit which had arrived a few days earlier. Two of the crew were killed including Squadron Leader Elsey the CO of the detachment. He was replaced by Flight Lieutenant Gellatly, RNZAF, who arrived, from Blida, on the following day.

In 17 March 1944, the Training Flight (TF), under the command of Flight Lieutenant Lapthorne (RAAF) was sent to Telergma where the Americans had their Bombardment Centre and where many Marauders were stationed. Thereafter the British squadron could more easily obtain spare parts from the Americans but the detachment still remained part of No.14 Squadron. At that time five B-26Bs were allotted to the TF leaving the Marauder Mk.Is for operational duty. Flight Sergeant Holland, the tail gunner in FK110/E, claimed a FW190 as damaged on 21 March 1944 and on the 29th another B-26B

Marauder FK156/C banking to the left shortly after taking off for another patrol sometime in the second half of 1943. By this time the Allies controlled most of the Mediterranean, and torpedoes were no more carried. (*Andrew Thomas*)

crew was lost. By that time the number of Marauder Is available was insufficient for operational needs and the Squadron had to use the B-26Bs to remain in action. By that time U-boat hunts and antisubmarine Patrols (ASP) comprised one third of all operational flights while the rest were the usual reconnaissance sorties. Within two days of the beginning of May the Squadron was hit hard when two more Marauders, FK120/X and FK110/E, were lost on operations, with the loss of twelve crewmen. They were partially revenged two days later when Flight Lieutenant Lantiga, RCAF, (FK145/N) was attacked by three Bf109Gs one of which was severely damaged while the other two were also hit. On the 13th Flying Officer MacDonald's crew (FK132/S), having inflicted two bursts of fire, claimed a Ju88 as damaged. It was the last claim reported by a Marauder Mk.I. Meanwhile training was continuing at Telergma and an accident occurred when on 22 May Lieutenant M. Overed, SAAF, with Sergeant Rawlings acting as second pilot crashed in FK118/TE. The aircraft was destroyed by fire, but the two pilots escaped uninjured.

On 8 June 1944 Wing Commander H. Law-Wright relinquished command to Squadron Leader E. Donovan. On 18 June, Flying Officer Hogg's crew was attacked (FK123/J) by two Bf109s which made three attacks on the Marauder. Hogg was able to take evasive action and, after 8 minutes, the enemy withdrew but the Marauder returned to base with many bullet holes in the airframe and both gunners wounded. On 26th, an attack was carried out, by two Ar 196s, on Flying Officer Roberston's aircraft (FK138/A) without inflicting any damage.

During June, the Squadron began to take on charge some replacement Marauders as some of the early models were decidedly war-weary. Furthermore, with various models in service maintaining the fleet was not an easy problem to resolve, especially as spare parts for the B-26As (Marauder Mk.I) were in short supply as this model was no longer flying in the States. Therefore the Squadron received one brand new Mk.II and some Mk.IIIs. During the month the Marauder Mk.I was gradually supplanted by the other models and while no more Mk.Is were lost the Squadron did lose two B-26Bs.

July began badly with the loss of another crew but the same month the situation changed in Europe with the success of the D-Day landings in Normandy. To support these landings it was decided to invade the south of France and the Squadron then began reconnoitring the north-west of Italy and southern France. However Marauder Mk.Is carried out only about half of the sorties flown in August and September. Nonetheless of six aircraft lost in August and September 1944 three were Marauder Mk.Is, including two on 13 September. FK109/W was damaged by Bf109s but the crew was safe, and FK124/L, whose crew were killed. On 21 September 1944 (FK138/X) crashed on takeoff and the crew were killed. Sadly, this was also the last day of No.14 Squadron's Marauder operations.

In two years, the Marauder Mk.I fleet had completed more than 8,000 operational hours in over 1,400 sorties. But by this date only 18 Marauder Mk.Is remained to be put into storage. This representing only 25% of the original total number of aircraft taken on charge by the RAF! Furthermore in excess 150 crewmen had been killed. The aggressive Commonwealth aircrews proved on many occasions that the Marauder Mk.I was a very good aeroplane. Even when flown in the unexpected roles of the maritime patrol and torpedo attack it recorded an impressive record.

Hubert Law-Wright served for two years with No.14 Squadron, eventually becoming its CO in August 1943, and was awarded the DFC and DSO before the end of the year. In June 1944 he was sent back to the UK for rest, before starting another tour of operations in January 1945. He commanded No.298 Squadron but sadly he and his crew, while flying in Halifax III NA660, failed to return from an SOE sortie on 3 April 1945. (*14 Squadron Association*)

Collyer's crew posing in front of FK145/N in 1943 :
Back, L to R : J.T. Collyer, J. Bradshaw and G.S. McKenna
Front, L to R : J. Eyre, R.W. Duke (RNZAF) and T.C. Climpson.

Donovan's crew in 1942 :
L to R : J.E. Stuart, M.C. Reid, G. Collins,
R.A. de Yarburgh-Bateson, R. Slatcher and E. Donovan

Lewis' crew in 1942 :
J. Bolton (RAAF),
from another crew
K.M. Dee (RAAF),
E.M. Lewis (SAAF),

H.C. Ridley,
an unknown groundcrew,
J.R. Sutton,
C. Locker

Philips' crew posing in front of FK151/O in 1943 :
O.A. Philips (RAAF), R. Osborne and A.R. Robertson
(RAAF) at far right. The three other are B.G. Foster, D.M.
Mackie and J.F.H. Scott, but their position on this photo are
unknown. Note the freshly painted "O".

Gellatley's crew in 1944 :
R. Slatcher, E.K. Stinger, W.R. Gellatly (RNZAF),
J.G. Watts, A.H. Laidlow and A.T. Harris.

THE OPERATIONAL RECORD

Marauder FK144/M flying at low altitude. Even if the Americans had used the Marauder against ships early in the war, the RAF was the only air force to have used the Marauder for shipping reconnaissance up to the end of 1944.
(via Peter H.T. Green)

OPERATIONAL DIARY - NUMBER OF SORTIES

Month	Sorties [1]	Hours flown [2]	Sqn Total Sorties	Sqn Total Hours
October 42	1	7.8	1	7.8
November 42	31	220.1	31	220.1
December 42	38	246.8	38	246.8
January 43	34	259.9	34	259.9
February 43	18	85.7	18	85.7
March 43	20	137.5	20	137.5
April 43	93	605.1	93	605.1
May 43	63	395.1	63	395.1
June 43	71	421.2	71	421.2
July 43	91	578.6	91	578.6
August 43	95	604.9	95	604.9
September 43	97	650.1	97	650.1
October 43	81	441.4	81	441.1
November 43	71	346.3	71	346.3
December 43	48	228.3	51	243.6
January 44	106	463.6	111	483.4
February 44	48	209.7	67	296.8
March 44	79	382.1	92	450.3
April 44	103	554.3	113	603.6
May 44	59	310.4	70	372.7
June 44	44	227.2	82	448.6
July	63	309.0	107	519.1
August 44	75	338.7	155	763.0
September 44	39	181.6	78	376.7
Grand Total	**1,468**	**8,205.4**	**1,730**	**9,558.0**

Extracted from AIR27/194-195

[1] Abortive take-off not included.

[2] Time for aircraft which failed to return is not included.

FIRST AND LAST SORTIE PLANNED

date	Mission	Serial	Time in/out
28.10.42	Met Recce	FK121/Y	0522-1313

Crew : Lt B.W. Young, Sgt E.A. Meadwell, P/O J.E. Foley-Brickley, P/O Barr, P/O K.J. Bennett, F/Sgt D.T. Ray, Sgt S.Hunt.

21.09.44	Recce	FK138/X	0445-crashed

Crew : W/O F. Elliott, Sgt A.K. Stewart, Sgt J.M. Khale, Sgt R.J. Heller, F/Sgt J.W. Bates, F/Sgt C.M. Taylor

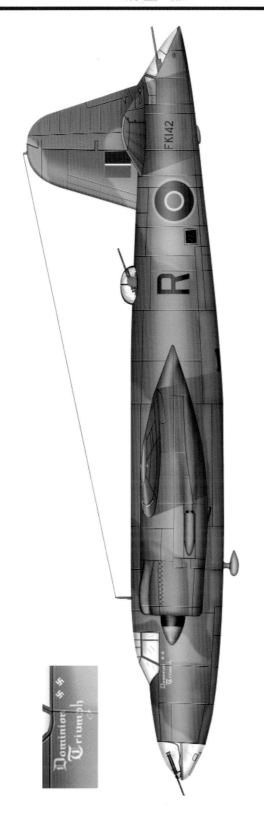

Martin Marauder Mk.I FK142 "Dominion Triumph", No.14 Squadron, Protville, Tunisia, August 1943.

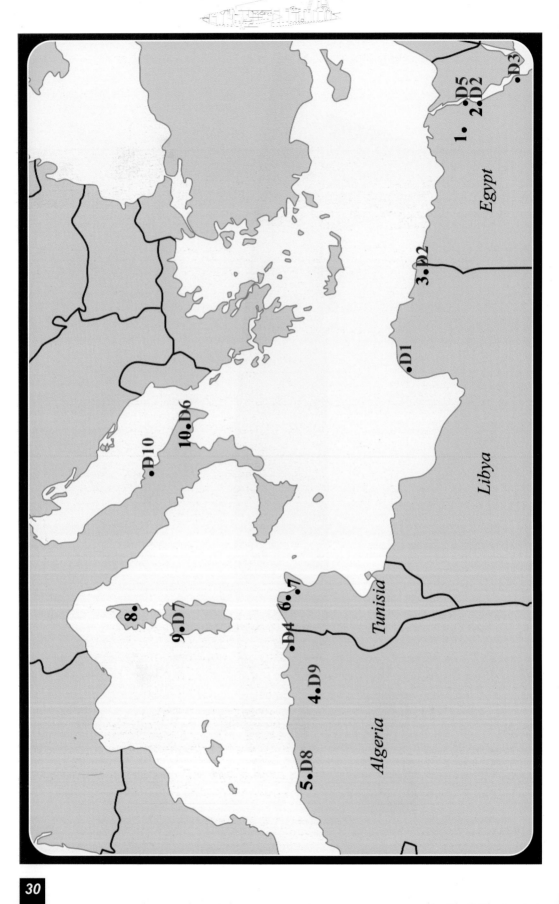

Two Marauders Mk.Is, believed to be at Blida, in North Africa in 1943. Note the Marauder in the background still painted in Desert camouflage. None are wearing an individual letter which suggests that they had just returned from a Maintenance Unit. (*ww2.images.com*)

MAIN MARAUDER MK.I BASES, MED 1942-1944

No.14 Squadron		Detachments (in red)
LG224 (West Cairo) [1]	09.08.42 - 25.08.42	-
Fayid [2]	25.08.42 - 23.02.43	Berka II (D1), Gambut 3 (D2), Shallufa (D3).
Gambut 3 [3]	23.02.43 - 01.03.43	Berka (D1), Shallufa (D3)
Telergma [4]	01.03.43 - 12.03.43	Berka III (D1), Gambut 3 (D2), Shallufa (D3)
Blida [5]	12.03.43 - 02.06.43	Gambut 3 (D2), Shallufa (D3), Bone (D4) Kasfareet (D5), Berka III (D1)
Protville I [6]	02.06.43 - 27.10.43	Bone (D4), Grottaglie (D6)
Sidi Amor [7]	27.10.43 - 05.12.43	Bone (D4), Ghisonaccia (D7), Grottaglie (D6)
Ghisonaccia [8]	05.12.43 - 13.01.44	Blida (D8), Grottaglie (D6)
Blida [5]	13.01.44 - 11.04.44	Grottaglie (D6), Ghisonaccia (D7), Telergma (D9)
Alghero [9]	11.04.44 - 23.09.44	Grottaglie (D6), Ghisonaccia (D7), Telergma (D9), Foggia (D10),
Grottaglie [10]	23.09.44 - 03.10.44	-

This Marauder is waiting for a new propeller and clearly shows the air intakes located on top of each engine cowling. From the very beginning the RAF used the much larger air intakes types, which appeared on the B-26B-1 model, as they could accommodate sand filters which the smaller intakes were unable to do. (*ww2.images.com*)

CLAIM LIST OF MARAUDER MK.I
(AGAINST AIRCRAFT)

Date	Pilot (& Gunners)	Type	Aicraft flown	Dest.	Prob.dest	Dam.
20.12.42	Sgt G.C. EGEBJERG, (Danish)	Bf110	FK131/E	1	-	-
	(Sgt D. Taylor, Sgt J.E. Allen)					
17.01.43	F/O O.A. PHILIPPS - RAAF	Ju52	FK159/W	-	-	0.5
	(Sgt G.M. Mackie, Sgt J.F.H. Scott)					
	Lt L.C. JONES - SAAF		FK120/X	-	-	0.5
	(Sgt J.B. Auckland - RAAF, Sgt A. Taylor)					
31.01.43	F/O H.S. GRIMSEY	Ju88		-	-	1
	(Believed to be F/O D.G. Bantham, Sgt D.G. McPail)					
19.04.43	P/O Robin K. FRANCIS	He115	FK123/J	-	-	1
	(F/Sgt I.D. Carnie, Sgt H.S. Mutch)					
20.04.43	F/Sgt K.M. DEE - RAAF	Ju88	FK130/F	-	-	1
	(Sgt C.B. Cray, Sgt H. Worthington)					
23.04.43	Sgt H.E. RAWLINS	Cant Z.501	FK121/Y	-	-	1
	(F/Sgt J. Liddle, F/Sgt J.H. Nuttall)					
28.04.43	F/L F.R. BROWN - RAAF	He59	FK130/F	-	-	1
	(F/Sgt W.G. Cavanagh - RAAF, Sgt L.C. Carr)					
15.05.43	Sgt H.E. RAWLINS	Ju52	FK145/N	-	-	1
	(Sgt J. Liddle, F/Sgt J.H. Nuttal)					
22.05.43	S/L H. LAW-WRIGHT	Me323	FK160/H	1	-	-
	(Sgt W.M. Cowie - RCAF, Sgt F.E. Lovelace - RCAF)					
10.06.43	F/O M.C JOHNSON - RAAF	Bf109	FK123/J	2	-	1
	(F/Sgt W.H. Hurstbourne, F/Sgt R.D. Gilbey)					
	F/Sgt H.W.T. BATES	SM82	FK159/W	1	-	-
	(F/Sgt J.P. Canavan, F/Sgt R.J. Davies)					
11.06.43	F/O E. DONOVAN	Bf109	FK147/B	1	-	-
	(F/Sgt G. Collins, F/Sgt J.E. Stuart)					
12.06.43	Lt R.K. GRAHAM, SAAF	Ju52	FK370/Z	-	-	1
	(Believed to be F/Sgt C.E. Campbell , F/Sgt C. Ewing)					
19.06.43	F/O M.C. JOHNSON - RAAF	Me210	FK159/W	-	-	1
	(F/Sgt W.H. Hurstbourne, F/Sgt R.D. Gilbey)					
15.07.43	W/C W.S.G. MAYDWELL	SM82	FK147/B	1	-	-
	(F/Sgt C. Locker, F/Sgt G.G. Graham)					
23.07.43	W/C W.S.G. MAYDWELL	Ju90	FK149/D	-	-	1
	(F/Sgt C. Locker, F/Sgt G.G. Graham)					
30.07.43	W/C W.S.G. MAYDWELL	Me323	FK142/R	1	-	-
	(F/Sgt C. Locker, F/Sgt G.G. Graham)					
	F/O H. ELSEY - RCAF	Ju52	FK156/O	-	-	3
	(Sgt D. Cradock, Sgt V. Aires)					
05.08.43	S/L H. LAW-WRIGHT	He111	FK162/H	-	-	2
	(Sgt W.M. Cowie, Sgt F.E. Lovelace, RCAF)					
06.08.43	F/O E. DONOVAN	Ju52	FK121/Y	-	1	-
	(F/Sgt D.G. Collins, F/Sgt J.E. Stuart)	FW190		-	-	2
07.08.43	F/O C.R. THOMSON - RCAF	Bf109	FK145/N	-	-	2
	(Sgt W. Camidge, Sgt A. Jamieson)					
18.09.43	F/O H. ELSEY - RCAF	Ju88	FK149/D	-	-	1
	(Sgt D. Cradock, Sgt V. Aires)					
19.09.43	F/Sgt F.M. SPEDDING - RNZAF	Re2001	FK149/D	-	-	1
	(F/Sgt E.W. Hills, Sgt W.L. Pollock)					

21.09.43	F/O D.F. **Thomas** - RCAF	Ju52	FK110/E	-	-	2
	(F/Sgt J.T. Fullerton, F/Sgt H.F. Morris)					
27.09.43	F/Sgt F.E. **Spedding**, RNZAF	Ar196	FK128/B	-	1	-
	(F/Sgt E.W. Hills, Sgt W.L. Pollock)					
04.11.43	F/O W.R. **Gellatly** - RNZAF	Bf109	FK126/P	-	-	1
	(Sgt A.T. Harris, Sgt A.H. Laidlaw)					
21.03.44	F/Sgt M.L. **Holland** - RNZAF	FW190	FK110/E	-	-	1
	(F/Sgt A.T. Smith - RAAF, F/Sgt K.J. Turner - RAAF)					
11.05.44	F/O S.R. **Lantinga** - RCAF	Bf109	FK145/N	-	-	1
	(F/Sgt R. Eaton, W/O P.D. Musto)					
13.05.44	F/O J.B. **MacDonald** - RCAF	Ju88	FK132/S	-	-	1
	(W/O2 J.R.P. Hogan - RCAF, F/Sgt A. Jamieson)					

<u>Total</u> : 8 aircraft destroyed, 2 probably destroyed and 28 aircraft damaged.

CLAIM LIST OF MARAUDER MK.I
(AGAINST SHIPS)

20.01.43   P/O J.H. **Elliott** - RAAF   800 ton   FK142/Y   1   -   -
Rest of the crew : F/O E. Donovan, F/Sgt C.R. Davies, F/Sgt C.H. Simmons, Sgt J.E. Stuart, Sgt K.J. Clarke

21.02.43   Major E.M. **Lewis** - SAAF   4,000 ton   FK370/Z   0.5   -   -
Rest of the crew : Sgt W.K. Bratt, P/O H.C. Ridley, Sgt J.H. Sutton, Sgt C. Locker , Sgt D.W. Sloggett
    F/O R.W. **Lapthorne**, RAAF   FK151/O   0.5   -   -
Rest of the crew : F/O A.J. Dolan, F/O D.L. Jones, F/O G.M. King, Sgt A. Ingham, Sgt D.D. Harris

    P/O G.W. **Clarke-Hall** - RAAF   5,000 ton   FK142/A   1   -   -
Rest of the crew : F/Sgt A.A. Caddell, P/O L.E. Parker, F/Sgt E.G. Clarke, F/Sgt R.E. Pollock, Sgt C.G.R. Heiden

Marauder FK109/W under repair at Alghero in 1944. Also under repair a Mosquito of No.256 Squadron and a French B-26G.
(14 Squadron Association)

AIRCRAFT LOST ON OPERATIONS

Date	Unit	Crew	SN	Origin	Serial	Fate
16.12.42	No.14 Sqn	Sgt Leonard A. EINSAAR	Aus.407318	RAAF	FK367/J	-
		Sgt Leonard R. DIXON	Aus.405577	RAAF		-
		Sgt Leslie B. WILLCOCKS	RAF No.1183698	RAF		-
		Sgt Tom E. EXELL	Aus.401305	RAAF		†
		Sgt Ralph I. PLOSKIN	RAF No.1186052	RAF		†
		Sgt Percival COCKINGTON	Aus.407707	RAAF		†
		Sgt Alan E. WATTS	RAF No.1301739	RAF		†
20.12.42	No.14 Sqn	P/O John T. WILLIS	RAF No.120485	RAF	FK366/S	PoW
		Sgt Samuel H. PORTEOUS	RAF No.1059847	RAF		†
		P/O Eric W. BARR	NZ402240	RNZAF		†
		P/O Peter B. MARTELL	RAF No.120866	RAF		†
		Sgt Frank BARRATT	RAF No.1076864	RAF		†
		Sgt Herbert F. FORD	Aus.401632	RAAF		†
03.01.43	No.14 Sqn	Capt B.W. YOUNG	No.103095	SAAF	FK375/D	PoW
		Sgt Edward A. MEADWELL	RAF No.1066549	RAF		†
		P/O James E. FOLEY-BRICKLEY	RAF No.126991	RAF		†
		P/O Kenneth J. BENNETT	Aus.401409	RAAF		†
		F/Sgt Dudley T. RAY	NZ403029	RNZAF		†
		Sgt Stanley HUNT	RAF No.1238830	RAF		†

Marauder FK375/D in 1942, in which Captain B.W. Young's crew was lost. *(IWM CM5001)*

Date	Unit	Crew	SN	Origin	Serial	Fate
15.02.43	No.14 Sqn	Lt L.C. JONES	?	SAAF	FK143/R	Int.
		F/Sgt John H.F. KELLY	RAF No.1375180	RAF		Int.
		W/O H.A. DUBE	CAN./?	RCAF		Int.
		F/Sgt Bevan J. MACK	Aus.407296	RAAF		Int.
		Sgt John B. ACKLAND	Aus.406546	RAAF		Int.
		Sgt A. TAYLOR	?	?		Int.
	No.14 Sqn	P/O Colin C. TRUMAN	Aus.402766	RAAF	FK150	†
		F/Sgt Jack I. THOMPSON	Aus.403437	RAAF		†
		F/O Bernard T. CONNELL	NZ402853	RNZAF		†
		F/Sgt Robert E.H. HOPE	Aus.407363	RAAF		†
		F/Sgt Kenneth FIRTH	RAF No.1068543	RAF		†
		F/Sgt William J. SEMPLE	RAF No.542705	RAF		†

Date	Sqn	Name	Service No.	Air Force	Aircraft	Fate
21.02.43	No.14 Sqn	Sgt Basil H. YARWOOD	RAF No.1067455	RAF	FK139/M	†
		Sgt Hamilton WALKER	RAF No.1063768	RAF		†
		F/Sgt Eric T.H. McCLEAN	RAF No.1058008	RAF		†
		F/Sgt Robert C. DAVIE	AUS.401618	RAAF		†
		Sgt Frederick GOTHERIDGE	RAF No.1147006	RAF		†
		Sgt Wiiliam J.E. GLENN	RAF No.1358073	RAF		†
	No.14 Sqn	Sgt Raymond A. BARTON	AUS.407612	RAAF	FK377/Y	†
		F/Sgt Norman A. McMILLAN	NZ411426	RNZAF		†
		P/O Robert H. ANNELLS	AUS.401292	RAAF		†
		Sgt George ARNOLD	AUS.407760	RAAF		†
		Sgt Frederick J. ARMSTRONG	RAF No.1292354	RAF		†
		Sgt Richard F. BELL	RAF No.1295359	RAF		†
12.04.43	No.14 Sqn	W/O Leonard A. EINSAAR	AUS.407318	RAAF	FK378/G	PoW
		Sgt R.A. KIRKIN	?	?		PoW
		F/O John C. BUCKLAND	AUS.401006	RAAF		PoW
		Sgt Thomas P. CLOWRY	AUS.402083	RAAF		PoW
		Sgt Leslie O. HARRISON	RAF No.927085	RAF		PoW
		Sgt John L. GOLDSMITH	RAF No.910986	RAF		†
24.04.43	No.14 Sqn	F/O Bruce S. SLADE	AUS.407674	RAAF	FK364/B	-
		F/Sgt Ernest F. BEDELL	RAF No.1376555	RAF		†
		F/O John B. MACDONALD	CAN./J.24184	RCAF		-
		F/Sgt Gilbert A. LINDSCHAU	AUS.407032	RAAF		-
		Sgt H.S. MUTCH	?	?		-
		Sgt Floyd E. LOVELACE	CAN./R.?	RCAF		-
25.04.43	No.14 Sqn	F/Sgt Thomas C. BULLOCK	RAF No.1379923	RAF	FK371/A	†
		W/O Frank L. TROVILLO	CAN./R.61964	RCAF		†
		P/O James L. MOUATT	RAF No.134353	(AUS)/RAF		†
		Sgt Colin WARBURTON	RAF No.1325781	RAF		†
		F/O Daniel G. BENTHAM	RAF No.114206	RAF		†
		F/Sgt James S. PATMAN	RAF No.1271098	RAF		†
09.05.43	No.14 Sqn	F/Sgt Thomas G.N. RUSSELL	AUS.400940	RAAF	FK155/V	†
		F/Sgt Peter FENNELL	RAF No.1194820	RAF		†
		W/O Francis V. DYSON	AUS.401007	RAAF		†
		F/Sgt Wiiliam J. NICHOLAS	AUS.401529	RAAF		†
		Sgt Joseph W. ARMSTRONG	RAF No.1078075	RAF		†
		Sgt Wallace H. AYTON	RAF No.1269886	RAF		†
26.05.43	No.14 Sqn	Sgt Henry E. RAWLINGS	RAF No.776183	RAF	FK160/H	-
		Sgt Wiiliam L. LUMSDEN	RAF No.1347766	RAF		-
		F/Sgt Leonard J. AUSTIN	RAF No.929361	RAF		-
		F/Sgt Edwin E. BURTON	AUS.405345	RAAF		-
		F/Sgt James H. NUTTAL	RAF No.1129545	RAF		-
		F/Sgt John LIDDLE	RAF No.943546	RAF		-
03.06.43	No.14 Sqn	Sgt Henry E. RAWLINS	RAF No.776183	RAF	FK112/L	†
		Sgt William L. LUMSDEN	RAF No.1347766	RAF		†
		F/Sgt Leonard J. AUSTIN	RAF No.929361	RAF		†
		F/Sgt Edwin E. BURTON	AUS.405345	RAAF		†
		F/Sgt James H. NUTTAL	RAF No.1129545	RAF		†
		F/Sgt John LIDDLE	RAF No.943546	RAF		†
27.06.43	No.14 Sqn	P/O Robin K. FRANCIS	RAF No.141729	RAF	FK363/G	†
		F/Sgt Richard G. MILES	NZ41925	RNZAF		†
		F/O Edward S. MURPHY	AUS.401171	RAAF		†
		F/Sgt Ian D. CARNIE	AUS.401492	RAAF		†
		F/Sgt Sydney G. JELLIS	RAF No.1188062	RAF		†
		F/Sgt Douglas W. SLOGGETT	RAF No.978473	RAF		†
24.07.43	No.14 Sqn	F/Sgt John D. HUNTER	AUS.400800	RAAF	FK147/B	PoW
		F/Sgt L.A. JOHN	RAF No.623529	RAF		PoW
		F/Sgt Richard EGAN	AUS.407525	RAAF		PoW
		F/Sgt Laurance M. MURPHY	AUS.401627	RAAF		PoW
		F/Sgt Maxwell F. STEPHENS	AUS.406664	RAAF		PoW
		Sgt R.V. JACKSON	RAF No.1432977	RAF		PoW

26.08.43	No.14 Sqn	F/O E.L. **ARCHER**	CAN./J.11465	RCAF	FK373/S	PoW
		F/Sgt A.R. **SMITH**	RAF No.1371351	RAF		PoW
		F/O John F. **KENNEDY**	RAF No.133779	RAF		PoW
		F/Sgt Gilbert A. **LINDSCHAU**	AUS.407032	RAAF		PoW
		Sgt J.T. **JONES**	?	?		PoW
		Sgt Alfred **PHETHEAN**	RAF No.978915	RAF		†
27.09.43	No.14 Sqn	F/Sgt Frank M. **SPEDDING**	NZ412275	RNZAF	FK128/B	-
		Sgt P.J. **BOWES**	RAF No.1558544	RAF		-
		Sgt Frederick A. **BROWN**	CAN./R.?	RCAF		-
		Sgt J. **STEPHENSON**	RAF No.1128877	RAF		-
		F/O George W. **HILLS**	RAF No.110472	RAF		-
		Sgt W.L. **POLLOCK**	raf No.1035562	RAF		-
19.10.43	No.14 Sqn	F/O Adam M. **CAMERON**	RAF No.108071	RAF	FK127/K	†
		F/O Geoffrey **INGRAM**	RAF No.116713	RAF		†
		F/Sgt David G. **WILLIAMS**	RAF No.1021766	RAF		†
		F/Sgt Colin V. **PROUD**	RAF No.621376	RAF		†
		Sgt Alastair I. **LESLIE**	RAF No.1340501	RAF		†
		Sgt H. **RITCHIE**	?	?		-
28.12.43	No.14 Sqn	F/O Richard W. **GILKEY**	CAN./J.11134	RCAF	FK133/A	†
		Sgt Henry E. **BRYCE-JEFFERY**	RAF No.778889	RAF		†
		W/O Robert A **BILLINGS**	CAN./J.86945	RCAF		†
		F/Sgt Alan B. **TUTTLE**	RAF No.553860	RAF		†
		W/O Charles Z. **TOUPIN**	CAN./R.131595	RCAF		†
		F/Sgt Donald A. **THOMSON**	CAN./R.99722	RCAF		†
01.02.44	No.14 Sqn	F/Sgt Maurice C. **REID**	RAF No.1130643	RAF	FK142/R	†
		F/Sgt John T. **BROWN**	RAF No.1314917	RAF		†
		W/O Arthur **WESTERN**	RAF No.968412	RAF		†
		F/Sgt Thomas N. **GILCHRIST**	RAF No.1122992	RAF		†
		F/Sgt Walter H. **CARR**	RAF No.1199387	RAF		†
		F/Sgt Patrick **DALEY**	RAF No.1028881	RAF		†
19.04.44	No.14 Sqn	F/O Herbert E.V. **BUDGE**	RAF No.128476	RAF	FK159/W	†
		F/O Oswald H.M. **HALL**	RAF No.138120	RAF		†
		W/O Donald K. **SCHRODER**	CAN/R.? *(J.86625)*	RCAF		†
		W/O Bernard J. **MACKINNON**	CAN./R.12153	RCAF		†
		W/O John M. **POWER**	CAN./R.? *(J.90045)*	RCAF		†
		W/O Allan **HUTTON**	CAN./R.?*(J.87713)*	RCAF		†
07.05.44	No.14 Sqn	F/O Arthur T. **SMITH**	RAF No.151054	RAF	FK120/X	†
		F/O Frederick J. **DELL**	RAF No.151603	RAF		†
		F/Sgt Orval P. **LAWSON**	CAN./R.? *(J.94370)*	RCAF		†
		Sgt Robert E. **ADDIS**	RAF No.1316695	RAF		†
		F/Sgt Walter W. **RICE**	RAF No.1212604	RAF		†
		Sgt Stephan **MCLENAGHAN**	RAF No.1046514	RAF		†
09.05.44	No.14 Sqn	Sgt John **ROSS**	RAF No.944914	RAF	FK110/E	†
		Sgt William M. **GREEN**	RAF No.1565841	RAF		†
		F/Sgt Alfred **WOODS**	AUS.420511	RAAF		†
		F/Sgt Edward J. **RYAN**	AUS.420601	RAAF		†
		F/Sgt Trevor **MACKRELL**	AUS.420694	RAAF		†
		F/Sgt Henry G. **ANDREWS**	RAF No.1332629	RAF		†
13.09.44	No.14 Sqn	P/O Alexander R. **HERSCHELL**	AUS.404176	RAAF	FK109/W	-
		F/Sgt Francis J. **HARRIS**	AUS.410170	RAAF		-
		F/Sgt Richard **ASHDOWN**	AUS.413507	RAAF		-
		W/O Richard **GASTEEN**	AUS.404912	RAAF		-
		F/Sgt Harold.A. **O'DONNELL**	AUS.410715	RAAF		-
		F/Sgt Keith G. **ROBERTSON**	AUS.425360	RAAF		-
21.09.44	No.14 Sqn	W/O Frank **ELLIOTT**	RAF No.1107012	RAF	FK138/X	†
		Sgt Alan K. **STEWART**	RAF No.1567845	RAF		†
		Sgt James M. **KAHLE**	RAF No.1545931	RAF		†
		Sgt Ronald J. **HELLER**	RAF No.1627009	RAF		†
		F/Sgt John W. **BATES**	RAF No.1238686	RAF		†
		F/Sgt Cyril M. **TAYLOR**	RAF No.1103542	RAF		†

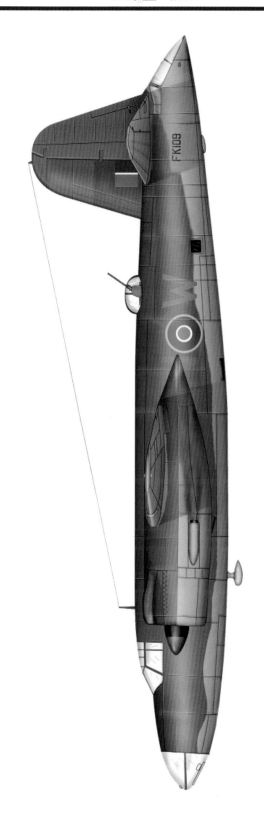

Martin Marauder Mk.I FK109, No.14 Squadron, Alghero, Sardinia, Summer 1944.

Aircraft Lost by Accident

Date	Unit	Crew	SN	Origin	Serial	Fate
19.07.42	Ferry Cmd	-	-	-	FK372	-
21.07.42	Ferry Cmd	*No details available on the crew*	?	?	FK158	-
17.08.42	Ferry Cmd	S/L Geoffrey **Robinson**	RAF No.40020	RAF	FK119	†
		Sgt George F. **Lyman-Dixon**	RAF No.1227812	RAF		†
		P/O James J.P.H. **Doran**	CAN./J.11496	RCAF		†
		Gordon H. **Randle**	-	Civ (Can)		†
20.08.42	No.14 Sqn	Col. Flint **Garrison**		USAAF	FK157	-
		P/O John T. **Willis**	RAF No.120485	RAF		-
27.10.42	Ferry Cmd	*No details available on the crew*	?	?	FK368	-
23.11.42	No.14 Sqn	F/O William R. **Bower**	CAN./J.8763	RCAF	FK122/P	†
		W/O2 Douglas L. **Rawson**	CAN./R.69358	RCAF		†
		F/O Peter McK. **Willis**	RAF No.118717	RAF		†
		Sgt Hugh G. **Williams**	RAF No.914350	RAF		†
		Sgt Edward **Cookson**	RAF No.987398	RAF		†
10.03.43	No.14 Sqn	S/L Peter **Goode**	RAF No.62010	RAF	FK154/K	†
		F/Sgt Reginald D. **Clapson**	RAF No.931143	RAF		†
		F/L Neville T.G. **Beacham**	Aus.405041	RAAF		†
		Sgt Victor **Brown**	RAF No.964042	RAF		†
		Sgt Clarnec V. **Walkinshaw**	RAF No.910071	RAF		†
		Sgt Leslie W. **Hunt**	RAF No.1387067	RAF		†
		F/O Henry M. **Siewart**	RAF No.101607	RAF		†
		F/Sgt Walter **Tatlow**	RAF No.356802	(CAN)/RAF		†
		LAC Donald V. **Bullen**	RAF No.649813	RAF		†
18.03.43	No.14 Sqn	Sgt Charles H. **Fletcher**	RAF No.1375522	RAF	FK117/C	-
		Sgt P.F. **Lynch**	?	?		-
		LAC John I. **Lewis**	RAF No.649703	RAF		†
10.05.43	No.5 METS	W/O Eric W. **McClelland**	RAF No.742489	RAF	FK376/H	†
		Sgt George B. **Wootten**	Aus.413065	RAAF		†
		Sgt Albert **Williams**	RAF No.1101199	RAF		†
		Sgt Leonard C.W. **Finlayson**	RAF No.778243	(SA)/RAF		†
		Sgt Eric E. **Blumfield**	RAF No.906029	RAF		†
		Sgt Robert C. **Quinney**	RAF No.1534949	RAF		†
		Cpl Wiiliam F. **Cooke**	RAF No.1360058	RAF		†
05.06.43	No.14 Sqn	F/Sgt Neville D. **Freeman**	NZ412675	RNZAF	FK134/P	-
		F/Sgt Robert O.B. **Fagan**	Aus.403690	RAAF		-
		F/Sgt Arvon A. **Jones**	Aus.401009	RAAF		-
		F/Sgt E.W. **Pearce**	?	?		-
		F/Sgt Henry G. **Hardy**	Aus.407500	RAAF		-
		Sgt Colin V. **Proud**	RAF No.621376	RAF		-
22.06.43	Ferry Cmd	Burton C. **Miller**	-	Civ (US)	FK129	†
		Lowell L. **Burchfield**	-	Civ (US)		†
		Reginald E. **Mudie**	Aus.403875	RAAF		†
		Philip A. **Vickery**	-	Civ (Can)		†

Marauder FK134 after its accident on 5 June 1943. *(ND Freeman via Paul Sortehaug)*

Date	Unit	Name	Number	Service	Aircraft	†
08.07.43	No.14 Sqn	F/O Anthony J. DOLAN	RAF No.118480	RAF	FK141	-
		Sgt Desmond B. EAGLE	RAF No.1335327	RAF		-
		Sgt Eric V.H. WEATHERLEY	RAF No.1172593	RAF		†
		Sgt Reginald M. PARRACK	RAF No.915144	RAF		-
		Sgt Derek D. HARRIS	RAF No.778734	RAF		-
		F/Sgt Reginald LODGE	RAF No.624121	RAF		†
		Capt Frederick W. BAYLISS*	-	-		†
		[*War Correspondent - Paramount News]				
10.07.43	No.14 Sqn	F/O Christopher P.M. PHILLIPS	RAF No.114395	RAF	FK152/S	†
		F/O Ernest J. BERTUCH	AUS.401294	RAAF		†
		F/Sgt Frederick V. PARKER	AUS.401629	RAAF		†
		Sgt Emlyn T.E. JONES	RAF No.1078253	RAF		†
		Sgt Daniel M.M. RICE	RAF No.1070428	RAF		†
		F/Sgt Frederick H. MASON	RAF No.1044965	RAF		-
		Sgt James T. COLLYER	RAF No.591185	RAF		-
20.07.43	No.14 Sqn	F/O Daniel F. THOMAS	CAN./J.9489	RCAF	FK374	-
		F/O Geoffrey A.A. CROSKELL	RAF No.133798	RAF		-
30.10.43	Ferry Cmd	*No details available, but no casualties reported*			FK116	
03.12.43	No.14 Sqn	F/L Ivor D.H. GIBBINS	RAF No.73054	RAF	FK370	-
15.12.43	No.14 Sqn	F/Sgt Frank R. TUXIL	RAF No.1312760	RAF	FK131/E	†
		Sgt Graham F. SIMPKIN	RAF No.1322793	RAF		†
		F/O Walter H. DAVIES	RAF No.130547	RAF		†
		F/Sgt Stephen G. THOMAS	RAF No.1314103	RAF		†
		W/O Wallace D. KEARNEY	CAN./R.115087	RCAF		†
		W/O Gordon L. READY	CAN./R.114466	RCAF		†

03.02.44 No.14 Sqn	P/O Sabo R. **Lantinga**	CAN./J.18233	RCAF	FK126/P	-
	P/O Charles A. **Duncan**	CAN./.J.21936	RCAF		-
	F/Sgt A.H. **James**	?	?		-
	W/O Roy H. **Mahood**	CAN./R.108639	RCAF		-
	F/Sgt Peter D. **Musto**	RAF No.1294764	RAF		-
08.02.44 No.14 Sqn	F/O Geoffrey A.A. **Croskell**	RAF No.133798	RAF	FK362/H	†
	Sgt Kenneth S. **Milford**	RAF No.1335353	RAF		†
	F/O John H. **Irwin**	CAN./J.21596	RCAF		†
	Sgt Arthur J. **Sims**	RAF No.1191722	RAF		†
	F/Sgt Percy **Ellenbogen**	RAF No.777876	(RH)/RAF		†
	F/Sgt Joseph E.J.B.G. **Lussier**	CAN./R.? *(J.90022)*	RCAF		†
	Sgt Thomas C. **Climpson**	RAF No.624799	RAF		†
23.02.44 No.14 Sqn	S/L Howard **Elsey**	CAN./J.9365	RCAF	FK130/F	†
	F/O Harry D. **Merkley**	CAN./J.10815	RCAF		†
	F/O Hudson C. **Campbell**	CAN./J.17252	RCAF		†
	F/O Allan C. **Bowes**	CAN./J.11214	RCAF		-
	F/O J.E.F. **Wright**	?	?		-
	Sgt **Bulbeck**	?	?		-
21.04.44 Training Flt	*No details available, but no casualties reported*			FK111/TV	
21.05.44 Training Flt	Lt Martin **Overed**	328310V	SAAF	FK118/TE	-
	Sgt Eric N. **Rowland**	RAF No.1458782	RAF		
13.09.44 No.14 Sqn	F/O Maurice T. **Holmes**	RAF No.161066	RAF	FK124/L	†
	P/O Philip M. **Todd**	RAF No.158759	RAF		†
	Sgt Cornelius S. **Keefe**	RAF No.1126779	RAF		†
	Sgt Walter H. **Ellis**	RAF No.1543941	RAF		†
	Sgt Mark **Irwin**	RAF No.1523165	RAF		†
	W/O William H. **Scourfield**	RAF No.1313686	RAF		†

Not all accidents ended by a write-off. On 16 May 1943, Pilot Officer O.A. Philips (RAAF), accompanied by Sergeant G.G. Foster, was asked to ferry FK365 from Bone to Blida for inspection. The aircraft belly landed due to a badly adjusted load which caused stability problems. The aircraft was repaired, but was never used in operations again and was eventually struck off charge on 30 November 1944. (*ww2images.com*)

Top : Front view of a Marauder displaying its short span wings. *(IWM CH17448)*
Centre : Close up of the nose. Note the stencil painted below the ground crewman's foot :
U.S.ARMY B-26A, AIR CORPS SERIAL NO-41-7379 , CREW WEIGHT 1000 LBS *(IWM CH17453)*
Below : Right side of FK130/F at Fayid in 1942. Note the faded fin flash and the US roundel under the wing !
(14 Squadron Association)

FY-41	Accepted	sub-type	RAF serial	Transferred to RAF	Airframe Hours	Modified	North Africa or UK
7345	31.10.41	B-26A	-	-	-	-	-
7346	31.10.41	B-26A	-	-	-	-	-
7347	31.10.41	B-26A	-	-	-	-	-
7348	31.10.41	B-26A	-	-	-	-	-
7349	31.10.41	B-26A	FK112	15.02.42	84.7	14.06.42	01.09.42
7350	25.11.41	B-26A	-	-	-	-	-
7351	25.11.41	B-26A	FK110	15.02.42	11.8	20.07.42	18.09.42
7352	25.11.41	B-26A	FK111	15.02.42	13.3	08.07.42	07.09.42
7353	25.11.41	B-26A	FK145	11.03.42	15.3	28.06.42	24.10.42
7354	25.11.41	B-26A	FK379	-	-	-	-
7355	25.11.41	B-26A	FK109	15.02.42	29.9	19.06.42	05.11.42
7356	25.11.41	B-26A	FK143	25.02.42	55.9	13.07.42	01.09.42
7357	25.11.41	B-26A	FK122	15.02.42	18.2	05.07.42	06.08.42
7358	31.12.41	B-26A	FK124	22.02.42	16.0	13.07.42	05.11.42
7359	31.12.41	B-26A	-	-	-	-	-
7360	31.12.41	B-26A	FK125	22.02.42	21.0	21.07.42	26.12.42
7361	31.12.41	B-26A	FK123	22.02.42	12.7	16.06.42	28.06.42
7362	31.12.41	B-26A	FK133	23.02.42	17.9	19.06.42	30.08.42
7363	31.12.41	B-26A	FK142	22.02.42	24.6	06.07.42	23.09.42
7364	31.12.41	B-26A	FK117	20.02.42	11.2	22.07.42	01.09.42
7365	31.12.41	B-26A	FK137	21.02.42	16.1	22.06.42	01.09.42
7366	31.12.41	B-26A-1	FK374	22.02.42	31.6	05.07.42	24.10.42
7367	31.12.41	B-26A-1	FK130	27.02.42	19.1	21.07.42	08.08.42
7368	31.12.41	B-26A	FK134	23.02.42	36.2	22.07.42	20.12.42
7369	31.12.41	B-26A-1	FK160	23.02.42	15.2	08.06.42	30.08.42
7370	31.12.41	B-26A-1	FK126	21.02.42	13.8	13.07.42	06.08.42
7371	05.01.42	B-26A-1	FK368	22.02.42	17.3	11.06.42	13.07.42
7372	31.12.41	B-26A-1	FK153	11.03.42	13.8	16.07.42	10.10.42
7373	31.12.41	B-26A-1	FK129	23.02.42	28.1	19.06.42	07.06.43
7374	31.12.41	B-26A-1	FK132	28.02.42	14.0	13.07.42	18.04.43

Marauder Mk.I Register

Career or comment and fate

Test aircraft Martin/Wright/Paterson/ Martin OMA. Written off 08.07.43.

Barksdale in September 1943. SOC 13.03.46 .

Barksdale 11.08.42 (17th BG, later 335th BG), Lake Charles 17.06.43, Barksdale (335th BG) 31.07.43, Keesler. SOC 13.03.46.

Barksdale 17.08.42 (17th BG), Eglin 16.12.42, Barksdale 31.12.42, Dodge City 02.07.43. *Class 26 - 01.09.43*. Scrapped 02.10.45.

On charge No.14 Sqn. Missing off Sardinia, 03.06.43.

Barksdale 30.06.42 (17th BG), MacDill 05.10.42, Dodge City 02.07.43. *Class 26 - 01.09.43*. Scrapped 13.03.46.

On charge No.14 Sqn. Missing from a recce mission over Adratic Sea, 09.05.44.

Sent UK arriving 07.09.42; Scottish Aviation 07.09.42; A&AEE 10.09.42; OAPU 31.05.43; No.301 FTU 03.08.43; No.1 OADU 14.08.43; dispoition MAC 15.08.43. No.14 Sqn.

On charge No.14 Sqn. SOC 29.03.45.

Was to have gone to RAF but wrecked before official transfer. Nose wheel failed to extend. Nashville, TN, 09.02.42. Destroyed Beyond Repair.

Sent UK arriving 05.11.42. AFDU 08.11.42; BDU 02.01.43; RAE 04.07.43; No.29 MU 03.06.43; No.1 OADU 06.03.44; No.304 FTU 10.06.44; disposition MAAF 22.06.44, No.14 Sqn.

Bellylanded Alghero after being attacked by Bf109s which caused damage to undercarriage, 13.09.44. SOC 30.11.44.

On charge No.14 Sqn. Force landing in Turkey. Interned, 15.02.43.

On charge No.14 Sqn. Tailplane broke off while manoeuvring on the bombing range, Shallufa, 24.11.42.

Sent UK arriving 05.11.42. A&AEE 28.11.42; No.1 OAPU 22.09.43; No.301 FTU 16.11.43 Disposition MAC 13.12.43. No.14 Sqn. Crashed on take off at night, Alghero, 13.09.44.

Barksdale 14.08.42 (17th BG). *Class 26 - 23.09.42.*

Crashed on ferry flight. No details available.

On charge No.14 Sqn. SOC 20.07.45.

On charge No.14 Sqn. Missing on operations, 28.12.43.

On charge No.14 Sqn. Missing on operations, 01.02.44.

On charge No.14 Sqn. Crashed while practising single-engine circuits, Fayid, 18.03.43.

Mainly used as trainer aircraft and liaison aircraft at the Squadron.

No details available. No.14 Sqn use unconfirmed.

On charge No.14 Sqn. Ran out of fuel on delivery flight to Protville and force landed in the western desert, 23 m from Tarkouna, Libya, 20.07.43.

On charge No.14 Sqn. Port engine failed during air test and crashed, Grottaglie, 23.02.44.

On charge No.14 Sqn. Tyre burst on landing during a transit flight, swung and broke back, Blida, 05.06.43.

On charge No.14 Sqn. Starboard mainwheel collapsed on landing on return from an operational recce at Bone, 26.05.43.

On charge No.14 Sqn. Mainwheel broke off and damaged port aileron and pitot head on take-off at Ghissonaccia for air test, 03.02.44. Destroyed during subsequent landing.

Lost in transit on 15.08.42. No more details available.

On charge No.14 Sqn. SOC 20.07.45.

Crashed into sea off Puerto Rico on ferry flight, 22.06.43.

On charge No.14 Sqn. SOC 26.04.45.

7375	31.12.41	B-26A-1	**FK127**	22.02.42	16.0	17.06.42	23.09.42
7376	31.12.41	B-26A-1	-	-	-	-	-
7377	31.12.41	B-26A-1	**FK150**	25.02.42	20.5	27.06.42	18.09.42
7378	31.12.41	B-26A-1	**FK144**	06.03.42	20.2	24.07.42	28.08.42
7379	31.12.41	B-26A-1	**FK138**	28.02.42	21.8	04.07.42	22.08.42
7380	31.12.41	B-26A-1	-	-	-	-	-
7381	31.12.41	B-26A-1	**FK135**	25.02.42	50.9	13.07.42	14.08.42
7382	31.12.41	B-26A-1	**FK114**	12.02.42	14.9	-	-
7383	31.12.41	B-26A-1	**FK113**	23.02.42	23.8	04.06.42	16.07.42
7384	31.12.41	B-26A-1	**FK116**	08.02.42	21.9	17.06.42	09.06.43
7385	31.12.41	B-26A-1	**FK121**	17.02.42	24.9	09.07.42	01.09.42
7386	31.12.41	B-26A-1	**FK118**	17.02.42	75.6	14.06.42	03.08.42
7387	31.12.41	B-26A-1	**FK139**	25.02.42	25.1	19.06.42	01.09.42
7388	31.12.41	B-26A-1	**FK141**	25.02.42	47.4	14.07.42	11.10.42
7389	31.12.41	B-26A-1	**FK119**	21.02.42	26.9	13.07.42	14.08.42
7390	31.12.41	B-26A-1	**FK120**	23.02.42	13.8	28.06.42	01.09.42
7391	31.12.41	B-26A-1	**FK115**	20.02.42	19.6	15.06.42	-
7392	31.12.41	B-26A-1	**FK377**	25.02.42	18.5	09.07.42	16.09.42
7393	31.12.41	B-26A-1	**FK128**	21.02.42	18.5	18.06.42	18.09.42
7394	31.12.41	B-26A-1	**FK146**	25.02.42	18.6	05.07.42	-
7395	31.12.41	B-26A-1	**FK131**	25.02.42	13.8	28.06.42	01.09.42
7396	31.12.41	B-26A-1	**FK375**	25.02.42	30.6	15.07.42	29.07.42 off
7397	31.12.41	B-26A-1	-	-	-	-	-
7398	31.12.41	B-26A-1	-	-	-	-	-
7399	31.12.41	B-26A-1	**FK159**	25.02.42	27.8	13.06.42	27.07.42
7400	31.12.41	B-26A-1	**FK136**	25.02.42	13.3	17.06.42	-
7401	31.12.41	B-26A-1	**FK148**	25.02.42	22.3	13.07.42	14.09.42
7402	31.12.41	B-26A-1	**FK147**	25.02.42	14.3	24.06.42	09.12.42
7403	31.12.41	B-26A-1	-	-	-	-	-
7404	31.12.41	B-26A-1	-	-	-	-	-
7405	31.12.41	B-26A-1	**FK365**	25.02.42	20.7	05.07.42	23.09.42
7406	31.12.41	B-26A-1	-	-	-	-	-
7407	31.12.41	B-26A-1	**FK372**	25.02.42	13.9	18.06.42	-
7408	10.03.42	B-26A-1	**FK371**	23.02.42	14.1	17.06.42	21.07.42
7409	19.03.42	B-26A-1	-	-	-	-	-

On charge No.14 Sqn. Crashed in Adriatic after aileron failure which caused uncontrollable turn to starboard, 19.10.43.

Barksdale 14.08.42 (17ᵗʰ BG), Dodge City (B-26 Transition School) 29.06.43. *Class 26 - 01.09.43.*

On charge No.14 Sqn. Missing on recce mission, 15.02.43.

On charge No.14 Sqn. SOC 20.07.45.

Arrived in UK 03.09.42. To C.R.D. (Controller of Research & Development) 05.09.42. No.20 MU 24.02.44. No.1 OADU 06.03.44. No.304 FTU for Middle East transfer 27.05.44. Under MAAF authority 05.06.44. No.14 Sqn. Hit cables on take-off and crashed at Grottaglie, 21.09.44.

Engine failure during touch and go and crashed 5 m SW of Glenn Martin facilities, Baltimore,MD, 29.01.42. 3 killed. Condemned 31.01.42.

On charge No.14 Sqn. SOC 20.07.45.

Tail structural failure in flight after the pilot's hatch escaped during test and crashed. Offutt Fd , NS, 25.05.42. 2 killed.

Lost during ferry flight. No details availble. Condemned 23.09.42.

Crashed near Accra (Gold Coast), 30.10.43. No further details.

On charge No.14 Sqn. SOC 29.03.45.

On charge No.14 Sqn, but also used by No.5 METS. Damaged beyond repair in accident during a training flight, 21.05.44.

On charge No.14 Sqn. Shot down by anti-aircraft fire during raid on Milos harbour, 21.02.43.

On charge No.14 Sqn. Swung on landing at Castel Benito and undercarriage collapsed, 08.07.43 at 11.55. Aircraft destoyed by fire. The aircraft was being ferried to Protville, Castel Benito being an intermediate stop.

Lost out of Natal during ferry flight 17.08.42.

On charge No.14 Sqn. Missing from a recce mission, 07.05.44.

Not much details available before December 1944. No.45 Group CS 16.12.44. SOC 12.07.45. Was on loan to Communication Sqn (Flight) of No.45 (Transport) Group at Dorval since 19.07.44.

On charge No.14 Sqn. Shot down by anti-aircraft fire during raid on Milos harbour, 21.02.43.

On charge No.14 Sqn. Heavily damaged by German aircraft during a shipping recce and crashed on landing at Protville, 27.09.43.

Crashed after suffering an in-flight stuctural break up, 07.08.42, 1.5 miles east of Keswick, VA, during ferry flight from Baltimore (Martin Corp), MD, to Nashville, TN. 2 killed.

On charge No.14 Sqn. Missing from navex, presumed crashed into sea, 15.12.43.

On charge No.14 Sqn. Missing from a torpedo armed recce in Aegian Sea. Attacked convoy Aghios Giorgios Islands. Believed shot down by escorting Bf110s, 03.01.43.

Used as test aircraft at Omaha (Martin Corporation), Patterson and Wright Flieds. *Class 26 - 16.08.43.* SOC 25.10.45

Damaged in accident 19.03.42. Repaired and used as test aircraft at Omaha (Martin Corporation), Patterson and Wright Fields. *Class 26 - 16.08.43.*

On charge No.14 Sqn. Shot down by fighter during a recce mission, 19.04.44.

Condemned 17.07.42. No more details available.

Condemned 26.09.42. No more details available.

On charge No.14 Sqn. Damaged by FW190s during recce and dictched into sea, 24.07.43.

Barksdale (17ᵗʰ BG) 19.07.42, Eglin 13.12.42, Barksdale (335ᵗʰ BG) 31.12.42, Eglin 31.01.43, Barksdale (335ᵗʰ BG) 11.03.43, Dodge City (B-26 Transition School) 29.06.43, Lowry Fd 30.08.43 as instructional airframe. Scrapped 02.10.45.

Baer Fd 04.06.42, Martin Corp date unrecorded, Baer Fd 02.10.42.

Crashed on take-off following loss of power on right engine, Lambert Fd, MO, 06.11.42. 1 killed.

On charge No.14 Sqn. SOC 30.11.44.

Barksdale (17ᵗʰ BG) 01.08.42, MacDill (21ˢᵗ BG) 04.10.42. *Class 26 - 23.10.43.*

Aircraft damaged during ground maintenance at Nashville, TN, 19.07.42. The aircraft was under 4ᵗʰ Ferry Group authority. *Class 26 - 29.07.42.*

On charge No.14 Sqn. Missing during a recce mission, 25.04.43.

Barksdale (17ᵗʰ BG) 22.06.42, MacDill (21ˢᵗ BG) 05.10.42. Left engine caught fire and gazoline spread over ship plane, MacDill, 10.02.43. SOC 10.07.43.

7410	19.03.42	B-26A-1	-	-	-	-	-
7411	25.02.42	B-26A-1	**FK149**	25.02.42	23.8	05.07.42	20.08.42
7412	26.02.42	B-26A-1	**FK151**	11.03.42	24.2	06.07.42	01.09.42
7413	06.03.42	B-26A-1	**FK373**	23.03.42	12.1	14.06.42	08.08.42
7414	25.02.42	B-26A-1	**FK156**	25.02.42	29.5	16.06.42	09.10.42
7415	25.02.42	B-26A-1	**FK363**	18.03.42	30.5	01.07.42	30.11.42
7416	09.03.42	B-26A-1	**FK157**	18.03.42	34.1	15.06.42	27.07.42
7417	12.03.42	B-26A-1	-	-	-	-	-
7418	25.02.42	B-26A-1	**FK140**	25.02.42	22.5	19.06.42	-

Marauder FK158 after its accident at Miami (FL) on 21 July 1942. Note the A1 type roundel. Many Marauder Mk.Is received these roundels before leaving the modification centre. They were later changed to the C1 pattern. (*Peter H.T. Green*)

7419	25.02.42	B-26A-1	**FK362**	11.03.42	16.9	05.07.42	11.10.42
7420	25.02.42	B-26A-1	**FK369**	25.02.42	22.0	11.06.42	-
7421	25.02.42	B-26A-1	**FK158**	18.03.42	16.1	11.06.42	-
7422	25.02.42	B-26A-1	**FK367**	18.03.42	26.1	17.06.42	01.09.42
7423	25.02.42	B-26A-1	**FK154**	23.03.42	22.3	04.07.42	01.09.42
7424	25.02.42	B-26A-1	**FK376**	25.02.42	14.2	17.06.42	01.09.42
7425	01.03.42	B-26A-1	**FK155**	09.03.42	44.7	19.06.42	01.09.42
7426	26.02.42	B-26A-1	*FK380*	-	-	-	-
7427	25.02.42	B-26A-1	-	-	-	-	-

Barksdale (335ᵗʰ BG) 01.12.42, Keesler 09.08.43 as instructional airframe. Scrapped 13.03.46.
On charge No.14 Sqn. SOC 29.03.45.
On charge No.14 Sqn. SOC 20.07.45.
On charge No.14 Sqn. Shot down by Ju52s during a recce off Sardinia and Corsica, 26.08.43.
On charge No.14 Sqn. SOC 29.03.45.
On charge No.14 Sqn. Missing during a recce mission, 27.06.43.
On charge No.14 Sqn. Hit truck on landing at LG224 (Cairo West) on returning from a trai-ning flight and crashed, 20.08.42.
Tarrant (B-26 Transition School) 31.12.42, Del Rio 23.02.43, Duncan Fd 25.02.43, Del Rio 17.03.43, Laughlin 07.07.43. Scrapped 21.12.44.
Left engine failed on take-off and crashed at the end of runway, Wright Field, 07.07.42. DBR. Condemned 27.07.42.

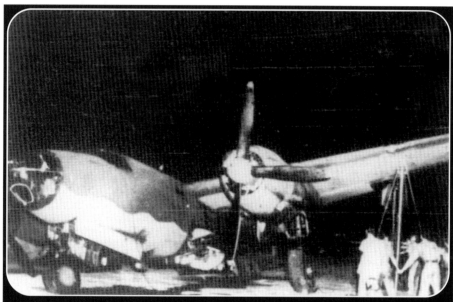

B-26A 41-7426 after its accident at Patterson (OH) on 21 March 1942. The aircraft was enroute to the modifi-cation centre where it would have become FK380 for the RAF. Unfortunately Patterson Field was the end of its short career. (*USAF*)

On charge No.14 Sqn. Crashed into sea during a transit flight to Blida, 08.02.44.
Condemned 25.07.42. No more details available.
Landing accident, Miami 21.07.42. *Class 26 - 31.08.42.*
On charge No.14 Sqn. Shot down by error by Malta-based Spitfires, 15 m of Benghazi, 16.12.42.
On charge No.14 Sqn. Crashed at 11.30 into Bay of Algiers, whilst transiting to Blida, 10.03.43. Possibly shot down by friendly fire from defenses of Algiers harbour while descending below clouds.
On charge No.14 Sqn, then used as trainer at No.5 METS. Crashed during a fighter affiliation flight on 10.05.43 at 9.30 hours. Tail broke off while circling Abu Sueir airfield crashing 2 miles SW of the place.
On charge No.14 Sqn. Missing during a recce mission, 09.05.43.
Was to have gone to RAF but wrecked before. Forced landing Patterson Fd, OH, 21.03.42.
Barksdale (17ᵗʰ BG) 24.06.42, Baton Rouge (21ˢᵗ BG) 09.08.42, Barksdale (335ᵗʰ BG) 15.09.42, Lowry Field 29.07.43. Survey 18.09.43.

7428	25.02.42	B-26A-1	**FK378**	11.03.42	25.7	07.06.42	01.09.42
7429	14.03.42	B-26A-1	**FK370**	23.03.42	31.5	17.06.42	28.07.42
7430	09.03.42	B-26A-1	**FK366**	18.03.42	38.0	22.07.42	01.09.42
7431	27.03.42	B-26A	-	-	-	-	-
7432	26.03.42	B26A-1	-	-	-	-	-
7433	10.03.42	B-26A-1	**FK364**	18.03.42	18.3	24.06.42	11.10.42
7434	10.03.42	B-26A-1	**FK152**	12.03.42	24.9	06.07.42	21.01.43
7435	11.03.42	B-26A-1	-	-	-	-	-
7436	10.03.42	B-26A-1	-	-	-	-	-
7437	10.03.42	B-26A-1	-	-	-	-	-
7438	10.03.42	B-26A-1	-	-	-	-	-
7439	10.03.42	B-26A-1	-	-	-	-	-
7440	12.03.42	B-26A-1	-	-	-	-	-
7441	21.03.42	B-26A-1	-	-	-	-	-
7442	13.03.42	B-26A-1	-	-	-	-	-
7443	12.03.42	B-26A-1	-	-	-	-	-
7444	19.03.42	B-26A-1	-	-	-	-	-
7445	26.02.42	B-26A-1	-	-	-	-	-
7446	26.02.42	B-26A-1	-	-	-	-	-
7447	26.02.42	B-26A-1	-	-	-	-	-
7448	11.03.42	B-26A-1	-	-	-	-	-
7449	20.03.42	B-26A-1	-	-	-	-	-
7450	14.03.42	B-26A-1	-	-	-	-	-
7451	12.03.42	B-26A-1	-	-	-	-	-
7452	02.04.42	B-26A-1	-	-	-	-	-
7453	14.03.42	B-26A-1	-	-	-	-	-
7454	13.03.42	B-26A-1	-	-	-	-	-
7455	14.03.42	B-26A-1	-	-	-	-	-

On charge No.14 Sqn. Attacked by two FW190s during a recce mission and ditched near Island of Ustica near Trapani, 12.04.43.
On charge No.14 Sqn. Nosewheel collapsed during run-up, Blida, at 10.40 on 03.12.43. Engine caught fire.
On charge No.14 Sqn. Exploded after being hit by anti-aircraft fire during a minelaying ope ration in Tunis harbour, 20.12.42.
Barksdale (17ᵗʰ BG) 20.07.42, Baton Rouge (21ˢᵗ BG) 13.08.42, Barksdale (335ᵗʰ BG) 12.09.42. *Class 26 - 03.11.42.*
Barksdale (17ᵗʰ BG) 21.06.42, Eglin 14.12.42, Barksdale (335ᵗʰ BG) 31.12.42, Tarrant (B-26 Transition School) date unrecorded, Barksdale (335ᵗʰ BG) 28.07.43, Keesler 08.09.43 as intructional airframe. Scrapped 13.03.46.
On charge No.14 Sqn. Damaged by FW190s and crashed on return at Tingley, Algeria, 24.04.43.
On charge No.14 Sqn. Starboard engine failed during air firing practice over sea and force landed at Bou Ficha at 10.30, 10.07.43. Aircraft destroyed by fire.
Barksdale (17ᵗʰ BG) 03.08.42. Landing accident, landing gear gave way, Barksdale 13.11.42.
Barksdale (17ᵗʰ BG) 25.06.42, Baton Rouge (21ˢᵗ BG) 09.08.42, Barksdale (335ᵗʰ BG) 19.09.42, Baton Rouge (21ˢᵗ BG) 15.10.42. Scrapped 13.03.46.
Barksdale (17ᵗʰ BG) 18.07.42, MacDill (21ˢᵗ BG) 05.10.42, Dodge City (B-26 Transition School) 06.08.43. *Class 26 - 01.09.43.* Scrapped 02.10.45.
Barksdale (17ᵗʰ BG) 20.07.42, Baton Rouge (21ˢᵗ BG) 13.08.42. *Class 26 - 04.09.42.*
Palm Beach 01.08.42, Tarrant (B-26 Transition School) 03.01.43, Del Rio 05.02.43, Stinson 20.03.43, Laughlin 10.05.43 - Mechanic School.
Chanute 20.07.42, Tarrant 31.12.42, Del Rio 06.02.43, Duncan 28.02.43, Del Rio 12.03.43. Scrapped 02.06.45.
Barksdale (17ᵗʰ BG) 01.08.42. Crashed 7 m NW of Little Rock, AR, 02.09.42. cause unknown. 6 killed.
Class 26 12.05.42. Returned to flying condition 31.01.43, Tarrant 04.02.43 (B-26 Transition School), Del Rio 05.02.43, Duncan Fd 26.02.43, Del Rio 07.01.43, Laughlin 22.07.43. Crashed 18 m S of Brooks Fd, TX, during an instrument training flight, cause unknown, 24.08.43. 4 killed.
Failure of nose wheel 17.05.42, Patterson, OH. Destroyed Beyond Repair.
Tarrant (B-26 Transition School) 17.12.42, Del Rio 05.02.43. Scrapped 03.01.46.
Barksdale (17ᵗʰ BG) 23.09.42, Baer 27.09.42, MacDill (21ˢᵗ BG) 04.12.42, Dodge City (B-26 Transition School) 08.07.43. *Class 26 - 01.09.43.* Scrapped 13.11.45.
Barksdale (17ᵗʰ BG & 335ᵗʰ BG) 27.09.42. Left engine caught fire in flight and crashed 3.5 m SW of Tenaha, TX, 16.01.43. 1 killed.
Barksdale (17ᵗʰ BG) 30.09.42. *Class 26 - 27.11.42.*
Barksdale (17ᵗʰ BG) 07.06.42, Baton Rouge (21ˢᵗ BG) 11.08.42, Barksdale (335ᵗʰ BG) 12.09.42 Stalled on approach on Barksdale Field, LA, and crashed, 20.10.42. 4 killed.
Barksdale (17ᵗʰ BG) 21.06.42, Baton Rouge (21ˢᵗ BG) 13.08.42, Barksdale (335ᵗʰ BG) 06.11.42, Dodge City (B-26 Transition School) 07.02.43. Scrapped 10.10.44.
Barksdale (17ᵗʰ BG) 25.06.42. Damaged 02.08.42. Not repaired. *Class 26 - 13.08.42.*
Barksdale (17ᵗʰ BG) 24.06.42. Crashed while tempting a force landing with the right engine dead at Lucas, 10 m south of Barksdale Fd, LA, 26.08.42. 4 killed.
Barksdale (17ᵗʰ BG) 07.06.42, MacDill (21ˢᵗ BG) 05.10.42. Crashed into Tampa Bay (FL), cause unknown during a transition flight, 13.03.43. 5 killed.
Barksdale (17ᵗʰ BG) 25.06.42. Damaged 02.08.42. Not repaired. *Class 26 - 06.08.42.*
Barksdale (17ᵗʰ BG) 22.06.42, Baton Rouge (21ˢᵗ BG) 13.08.42, Barksdale (335ᵗʰ BG) 28.03.43, Dodge City (B-26 Transition School) 13.07.43. *Class 26 - 01.09.43.*
Barksdale (17ᵗʰ BG) 27.06.42, Baton Rouge (21ˢᵗ BG) 09.08.42, Barksdale (335ᵗʰ BG) 15.09.42. Crashed while trying to make a force landing with the right engine cut, 26.04.43, 1 m S of Braksdale Fd. 1 killed.

7456	14.03.42	B-26A-1	-	-	-	-	-
7457	11.03.42	B-26A-1	-	-	-	-	-
7458	18.03.42	B-26A-1	-	-	-	-	-
7459	13.03.42	B-26A-1	-	-	-	-	-
7460	11.03.42	B-26A-1	-	-	-	-	-
7461	19.03.42	B-26A-1	-	-	-	-	-
7462	12.03.42	B-26A-1	-	-	-	-	-
7463	18.03.42	B-26A-1	-	-	-	-	-
7464	21.03.42	B-26A-1	-	-	-	-	-
7465	23.03.42	B-26A-1	-	-	-	-	-
7466	19.03.42	B-26A-1	-	-	-	-	-
7467	16.03.42	B-26A-1	-	-	-	-	-
7468	23.03.42	B-26A-1	-	-	-	-	-
7469	29.03.42	B-26A-1	-	-	-	-	-
7470	20.03.42	B-26A-1	-	-	-	-	-
7471	02.04.42	B-26A-1	-	-	-	-	-
7472	26.03.42	B-26A-1	-	-	-	-	-
7473	26.03.42	B-26A-1	-	-	-	-	-
7474	02.04.42	B-26A-1	-	-	-	-	-
7475	27.03.42	B-26A-1	-	-	-	-	-
7476	23.03.42	B-26A-1	-	-	-	-	-
7477	09.04.42	B-26A	-	-	-	-	-
7478	25.03.42	B-26A	-	-	-	-	-
7479	26.03.42	B-26A	-	-	-	-	-
7480	02.04.42	B-26A	-	-	-	-	-
7481	05.04.42	B-26A	-	-	-	-	-
7482	05.04.42	B-26A	-	-	-	-	-
7483	07.04.42	B-26A	-	-	-	-	-

Landing gear failure, 31.03.42 Patterson Fd, OH. Became instructional Airframe at Sheppard 04.05.42. Scrapped 13.10.44.

Barksdale (17ᵗʰ BG) 26.07.42. *Class 26 - 10.09.42.*

Barksdale (17ᵗʰ BG) 25.06.42. No further details. SOC 19.10.45.

Barksdale (17ᵗʰ BG) 25.06.42. Pilot lost control while simulating a engine failure, dove and crashed 4 m W of Plain Dealing, LA, 20.09.42. 3 killed. Condemned 24.09.42.

Barksdale (17ᵗʰ BG) 15.09.42, Dodge City (B-26 Transition School) 17.09.42. *Class 26 - 01.09.43.*

Barksale (17ᵗʰ BG) 23.06.42, MacDill (21ˢᵗ BG) 04.10.42. Crashed in Tampa Bay, 4 m WNW of MacDill Fd, FL, cause unknown, 10.04.43. 5 killed.

Barksdale (17ᵗʰ BG) 27.06.42 MacDill (21ˢᵗ BG) 04.10.42, Scott 09.11.42, MacDill (21ˢᵗ BG) 12.01.43, Lakeland (335ᵗʰ BG) 08.04.43, MacDill (21ˢᵗ BG) 06.04.43, Buckley 12.08.43 as instructional airframe. Scrapped 20.03.46.

Barksdale (17ᵗʰ BG) 24.06.42. Condemned 28.08.42.

Barksdale (17ᵗʰ BG) 26.06.42, Baton Rouge (21ˢᵗ BG) 13.08.42, Barksdale (335ᵗʰ BG) 27.02.43, Dodge City (B-26 Transition School) 19.07.43. *Class 26 - 01.09.43.*

Barksdale (17ᵗʰ BG) 26.06.42, Dodge City (B-26 Transition School) 14.07.43. *Class 26 - 01.09.43.* Scrapped 26.09.44

Barksdale (17ᵗʰ BG) 26.06.42. Condemned 08.09.42.

Barksdale (17ᵗʰ BG) 23.06.42. Wrecked after hatch blew off on take off. Pilot landed on belly, Barksdale, LA, 05.06.42. *Class 26 - 14.07.42.*

Barksdale (17ᵗʰ BG) 24.06.42, Baton Rouge 09.08.42, Dodge City (B-26 Transition School) 07.07.43. *Class 26 - 01.09.43.* Scrapped 02.10.45.

Barksdale (17ᵗʰ BG) 24.06.42, MacDill (21ˢᵗ BG) 04.10.42. Crashed on landing at MacDill Fd (FL) after left engine caught fire in flight, 16.04.43. 3 killed.

Barksdale (17ᵗʰ BG) 21.06.42, Baton Rouge 13.08.42, Barksdale (335ᵗʰ BG) 18.09.42, Bryan 19.05.43, Barksdale (335ᵗʰ BG) 22.07.43, Lowry 20.07.43 as Instructional airframe. Scrapped 02.10.45.

Barksdale (17ᵗʰ BG) 15.07.42, Eglin 14.12.42, Barksdale (335ᵗʰ BG) 31.12.42. Sheppeard 26.02.43 as Instructional airframe. Scrapped 13.10.44.

Barksdale (17ᵗʰ BG) 25.06.42, Baton Rouge 09.08.42, Barksdale (335ᵗʰ BG) 15.10.42. Force landing in a plowed field near Barksdale Field, LA, 25.04.43. *Class 26 - 02.05.43* at Sheppard Field.

Barksdale (17ᵗʰ BG) 22.08.42, MacDill 04.10.42. Wrecked 2 miles of Gandy Bridge in Tampa Bay, FL, cause unknown, 20.10.42.

Charlotte15.04.42, Barksdale (17ᵗʰ BG) 01.08.42, Dodge City (B-26 Transition School) 28.06.43. *Class 26 - 01.09.43.* Scrapped 05.12.44.

Barksdale (17ᵗʰ BG) 28.06.42. Stalled and dove into ground on training flight 1 m W of Abington, LA, 02.07.43. 5 killed. Condemned 04.04.43.

Barksdale (17ᵗʰ BG) 24.06.42. *Class 26 - 16.07.42*

Barksdale (17ᵗʰ BG) 01.08.42, MacDill (21ˢᵗ BG) 07.10.42. Crashed on 31.05.43 at Pradentown, FL, during a training flight, cause unknown. 5 killed.

Barksdale (17ᵗʰ BG) 06.07.42, MacDill (21ˢᵗ BG) 05.10.42, Lakeland 31.05.43, MacDill (336ᵗʰ BG) 10.07.43. No more details available.

Barksdale (17ᵗʰ BG) 21.06.42. Condemned 12.08.42.

Barksdale (17ᵗʰ BG) 30.06.42, Baton Rouge 09.08.42. Crashed 5 m South of Bogalusa, LA, during an instrumental training flight, 23.08.42. 6 killed. Condemned 11.09.42.

Barksdale (335ᵗʰ BG) 01.10.42, Keesler Fd as instructional airframe 04.08.43. Scrapped 26.09.44.

Barksdale (17ᵗʰ BG) 30.06.42. Stalled, spinned and dove into the ground, 10 m West of Barksdale Fd, 25.05.42. 4 killed.

Barksdale (17ᵗʰ BG) 29.06.42, Baton Rouge 09.08.42. Crashed 01.09.42 near Angola, LA, following a right engine fire. 7 killed. Scrapped 07.11.42.

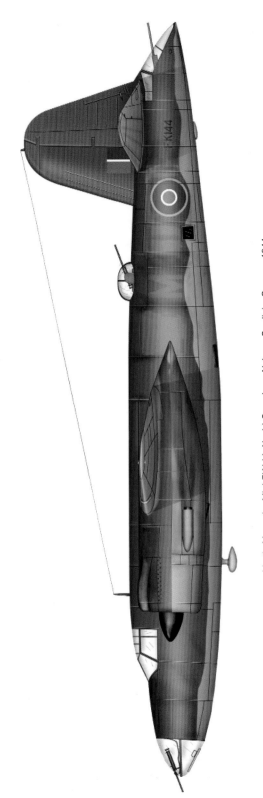

Martin Marauder Mk.I FK144, No.14 Squadron, Alghero, Sardinia, Summer 1944.
Note the size of the fuselage roundel which replaced the oversized version in 1944.
Also, a shadow of a "T" of the Training Flight can be noted under the patch of new paint between the individual letter and the roundel. It is not certain it was the rule for all aircraft of the Training Flight, but that gives an indication.

Known number of sortie completed by each No.14 Squadron's Marauder Mk.Is

Serial	Individual letter	First sortie	Last sortie	Total	Op.hours	Comment
FK109	W	10.07.44	23.08.44	21	102.3	
FK110	E	06.07.43	06.05.44	49	298.6	Lost on its 50th sortie
FK111	V & TV	23.10.43	03.04.44	27	121.2	
FK112	L & E	01.11.42	29.05.43	9	64.1	Lost on its 10th sortie
FK117	G	08.02.43	08.02.43	1	9.1	
FK118	N/TE	-	-	-	-	
FK120	X	10.11.42	06.05.44	82	526.8	Lost on its 83rd sortie
FK121	Y	28.10.42	17.06.44	53	289.1	
FK122	P	03.11.42	20.11.42	2	12.5	
FK123	J & T	21.02.43	18.09.44	125	685.0	
FK124	Z & L	19.03.44	10.09.44	24	120.5	Lost on its 25th sortie
FK126	C & P	16.12.42	24.01.44	57	326.5	
FK127	K	26.08.43	15.10.43	12	56.5	Lost on its 13th sortie
FK128	U & B	08.04.43	27.09.43	10	60.8	
FK130	F	06.11.42	30.07.43	35	201.9	
FK131	E	07.11.42	19.12.42	8	55.7	
FK132	S	08.09.43	14.09.44	76	360.7	
FK133	R, J & A	19.12.42	15.11.43	13	70.3	Lost on its 14th sortie
FK134	P	-	-	-	-	
FK135	P	02.03.44	12.09.44	22	101.6	
FK138	X	26.06.44	09.09.44	41	191.5	Lost on its 42nd sortie
FK139	M	09.01.43	09.01.43	1	2.5	Lost on its 2nd sortie
FK141	?	-	-	-	-	
FK142	O, Z, Y & R	03.01.43	30.01.44	45	280.7	Lost on its 46th sortie
FK143	R	22.11.42	26.01.43	4	31.5	Lost on its 5th sortie
FK144	A, M & TM	27.03.43	15.09.44	95	525.8	
FK145	N	29.04.43	11.09.44	65	365.8	
FK147	B	15.05.43	22.07.43	17	104.9	Lost on its 18th sortie
FK149	D & O	21.02.43	08.08.44	103	565.4	
FK150	?	15.02.43	-	-	-	Lost on its 1st sortie
FK151	O & TO	03.11.42	02.06.44	45	273.8	
FK152	S	-	-	-	-	
FK153	Q & P	31.12.42	24.07.44	42	220.6	
FK154	K	09.11.42	02.04.43	6	43.8	
FK155	V	09.11.42	06.05.43	5	36.6	Lost on its 6th sortie
FK156	C	01.07.43	15.09.44	73	388.3	
FK157	?	-	-	-	-	
FK159	B & W	16.11.42	12.04.44	80	479.7	Lost on its 81st sortie
FK160	P & H	18.01.43	21.05.43	12	86.8	
FK362	H	05.06.43	21.01.44	40	185.9	
FK363	G	21.05.43	26.06.44	7	44.3	Lost on its 8th sortie
FK364	B	26.03.43	23.04.43	9	64.2	Lost on its 10th sortie
FK365	U	-	-	-	-	
FK366	S	03.11.42	06.12.42	3	28.9	Lost on its 4th sortie
FK367	J	02.11.42	16.12.42	5	33.3	Lost on its 6th sortie
FK370	Z & L	10.11.42	10.11.43	33	233.0	
FK371	A	10.12.42	18.04.43	15	104.3	Lost on its 16th sortie
FK373	S	26.03.43	21.08.43	30	205.8	Lost on its 31st sortie
FK375	D	06.11.42	01.01.43	3	21.0	Lost on its 4th sortie
FK376	H	02.11.42	09.01.43	4	31.7	
FK377	Y	21.02.43	-	-	-	Lost on its 1st sortie
FK378	G	21.01.43	10.04.43	8	54.4	Lost on its 9th sortie

Notes :
Missing from this total are 28 sorties and 138.1 operational hours which cannot be identified with any certainty.
Some aircraft were used only for training duties. By April 1943 an official training flight was formed; its aircraft were identified with a "T" painted before or after the individual letter. But the size, location and colour of the "T" is not known.
(see also profile on the opposite page)

ROLL OF HONOUR

MARAUDER MK.I

Name	Rank (as CWGC)	Age	Origin	Date	Serial
ADDIS, Robert Edwin	Sgt	20	RAF	07.05.44	FK120
ANDREWS, Henry George	F/Sgt	22	RAF	09.05.44	FK110
ANNELLS, Robert Harvey	P/O	26	RAAF	21.02.43	FK377
ARMSTRONG, Frederick John	Sgt	22	RAF	21.02.43	FK377
ARMSTRONG, Joseph Walter	Sgt	29	RAF	09.05.43	FK155
ARNOLD, George	Sgt	27	RAAF [1]	21.02.43	FK377
AUSTIN, Leonard John	F/Sgt	n/a	RAF	03.06.43	FK112
AYTON, Wallace Henry	Sgt	21	RAF	09.05.43	FK155
BARR, Eric William	P/O	25	RNZAF	20.12.42	FK366
BARRATT, Frank	Sgt	31	RAF	20.12.42	FK366
BARTON, Raymond Allan	Sgt	29	RAAF	21.02.43	FK377
BATES, John William	F/Sgt	33	RAF	21.09.44	FK138
BAYLISS, Frederick William	Capt	31	*War Cor.*	08.07.43	FK141
BEACHAM, Neville Thomas George	F/L	27	RAAF [2]	10.03.43	FK154
BEDELL, Ernest Frederick	Sgt	30	RAF	24.04.43	FK364
BELL, Richard Frederick	Sgt	21	RAF	21.02.43	FK377
BENNETT, Kenneth Jack	P/O	25	RAAF	03.01.43	FK375
BENTHAM, Daniel Gerald	F/O	33	RAF	25.04.43	FK371
BERTUCH, Ernest James	F/O	34	RAAF	10.07.43	FK152
BILLINGS, Robert Arnold	P/O	25	RCAF	28.12.43	FK133
BLUMFIELD, Eric Emlyn	Sgt	n/a	RAF	10.05.43	FK376
BOWER, William Richardson	F/O	31	RCAF	23.11.42	FK122
BROWN, John Thomas	F/Sgt	n/a	RAF	01.02.44	FK142
BROWN, Victor	Sgt	n/a	RAF	10.03.43	FK154
BRYCE-JEFFERY, Henry Edmund	Sgt	n/a	RAF	28.12.43	FK133
BUDGE, Herbert Eric Victor	F/O	23	RAF	19.04.44	FK159
BULLEN, Donald Victor	LAC	21	RAF	10.03.43	FK154
BULLOCK, Thomas Carolus	F/Sgt	n/a	RAF	25.04.43	FK371
BURTON, Edwin E.	F/Sgt	n/a	RAAF	03.06.43	FK112
BURCHFIELD, Lowell Luther	-	n/a	*Civil/US*	22.06.43	FK129
CAMERON, Adam Mitchell	F/O	29	RAF	19.10.43	FK127
CAMPBELL, Hudson Cecil	F/O	22	RCAF	23.02.44	FK120
CARNIE, Ian David	F/Sgt	22	RAAF	27.06.43	FK363
CARR, Walter Horace	F/Sgt	19	RAF	01.02.44	FK142
CLAPSON, Reginald Arthur	F/Sgt	21	RAF	10.03.43	FK154
CLEMENS, Kenneth G.	-	37	*Civil/US*	07.08.42	FK146
CLIMPSON, Thomas Charles	Sgt	n/a	RAF	08.02.44	FK362
COCKINGTON, Percival	Sgt	21	RAAF	16.12.42	FK367
CONNELL, Bernard Thomas	F/O	25	RNZAF	15.02.43	FK150
COOKE, William Frederick	Cpl	33	RAF	10.05.43	FK376

[1] English-born Australian
[2] Welsh-born Australian

COOKSON, Ernest	Sgt	25	RAF	23.11.42	FK122
CROSKELL, Geoffrey Arthur Austin	F/O	25	RAF	08.02.44	FK362
DALEY, Patrick	W/O	21	RAF	01.02.44	FK142
DAVIE, Robert Curtis	F/Sgt	25	RAAF	21.02.43	FK139
DAVIES, Walter Houghton	F/O	n/a	RAF	15.12.43	FK131
DELL, Frederick John	F/O	22	RAF	07.05.44	FK120
DORAN, James John Pierre Hector	P/O	n/a	RCAF	17.08.42	FK119
DYSON, Francis Victor	W/O	29	RAAF	09.05.43	FK155
ELLENBOGEN, Percy	F/Sgt	n/a	(RH)/RAF	08.02.44	FK362
ELLIOTT, Frank	P/O	24	RAF	21.09.44	FK138
ELLIS, Walter Hubert	Sgt	23	RAF	13.09.44	FK124
ELSEY, Howard	S/L	n/a	RCAF	23.02.44	FK130
EXELL, Tom Ellis	Sgt	21	RAAF	16.12.42	FK367
FENNELL, Peter	F/Sgt	20	RAF	09.05.43	FK155
FINLAYSON, Leonard Colin Wynne	Sgt	25	(SA)/RAF	10.05.43	FK376
FIRTH, Kenneth	F/Sgt	22	RAF	15.02.43	FK150
FOLEY-BRICKLEY, James Ernest	F/O	n/a	RAF	03.01.43	FK375
FORD, Herbert Frank	Sgt	27	RAAF	20.12.42	FK366
FRANCIS, Robin Keith	P/O	n/a	RAF	27.06.43	FK363
GILCHRIST, Thomas Norman	F/Sgt	20	RAF	01.02.44	FK142
GILKEY, Richard Wallace	F/O	n/a	RCAF	28.12.43	FK133
GLENN, William John Ernest	Sgt	n/a	RAF	21.02.43	FK139
GOLDSMITH, John Lewis	F/Sgt	22	RAF [3]	12.04.43	FK378
GOODE, Peter	S/L	21	RAF	10.03.43	FK154
GOTHERIDGE, Frederick	Sgt	21	RAF	21.02.43	FK139
GREEN, William Macmillan	Sgt	20	RAF	09.05.44	FK110
HALL, Oswald Henry Mark	F/O	31	RAF	19.04.44	FK159
HARTLEY, Carl W.	-	30	*Civil/US*	25.05.42	FK114
HELLER, Ronald Joseph	Sgt	20	RAF	21.09.44	FK138
HOLMES, Maurice Trevor	F/O	28	RAF	13.09.44	FK124
HOPE, Robert Edward Herbert	F/Sgt	33	RAAF	15.02.43	FK150
HUNT, Leslie William	F/Sgt	22	RAF	10.03.43	FK154
HUNT, Stanley	Sgt	n/a	RAF	03.01.43	FK375
HUTTON, Allan	W/O	24	RCAF	19.04.44	FK159
INGRAM, Geoffrey	F/O	24	RAF	19.10.43	FK127
IRWIN, John Howard	F/O	22	RCAF	08.02.44	FK362
IRWIN, Mark	Sgt	21	RAF	13.09.44	FK124
JELLIS, Sydney Gordon	F/Sgt	29	RAF	27.06.43	FK363
JONES, Emlyn Thomas Enoch	Sgt	28	RAF	10.07.43	FK152
KAHLE, James Michael	Sgt	23	RAF	21.09.44	FK138
KEARNEY, Wallace David	W/O2	19	RCAF	15.12.43	FK131
KEEFE, Cornelius Swinnerton	Sgt	28	RAF	13.09.44	FK124
LAWSON, Orval Percy	P/O	27	RCAF	07.05.44	FK120
LESLIE, Alastair Ian	Sgt	23	RAF	19.10.43	FK127
LEWIS, John Irfon	LAC	21	RAF	18.03.43	FK117
LIDDLE, John	F/Sgt	22	RAF	03.06.43	FK112
LODGE, Reginald	F/Sgt	22	RAF	08.07.43	FK141
LUMSDEN, William Lister	Sgt	21	RAF	03.06.43	FK112
LUSSIER, Joseph Emile Jean Baptiste G.	P/O	22	RCAF	08.02.44	FK362
LYMAN-DIXON, George Frederick	Sgt	28	RAF	17.08.42	FK119
MACKINNON, Bernard Joseph	W/O	n/a	RCAF	19.04.44	FK159
MACKRELL, Trevor	F/Sgt	22	RAAF	09.05.44	FK110
McCLEAN, Eric Thomas Harold	F/Sgt	24	RAF	21.02.43	FK139
McLENAGHAN, Stephan	Sgt	22	RAF	07.05.44	FK120

[3] Native of the Channel Islands, at that time occupied by the Germans

McCLELLAND, Eric Walker	P/O	28	RAF	10.05.43	FK376
McMILLAN, Norman Archibald	F/Sgt	26	RNZAF	21.02.43	FK377
MARTELL, Peter Benson	F/O	21	RAF	20.12.42	FK366
MEADWELL, Edward Arthur	Sgt	30	RAF	03.01.43	FK375
MERKLEY, Harry Dwain	F/O	22	RCAF	23.02.44	FK130
MEYERS, Henry K.	-	24	*Civil/US*	25.05.42	FK114
MILES, Richard George	F/Sgt	21	RNZAF	27.06.43	FK363
MILFORD, Kenneth Sydney	Sgt	20	RAF	08.02.44	FK362
MILLER, Burton Craig	-	n/a	*Civil/US*	22.06.43	FK129
MOUATT, James Leslie	F/O	22	(AUS)/RAF	25.04.43	FK371
MUDIE, Reginald Edward	W/O2	25	RAAF	22.06.43	FK129
MURPHY, Edward Scott	F/O	26	RAAF [1]	27.06.43	FK363
NICHOLAS, William James	F/Sgt	31	RAAF	09.05.43	FK155
NUTTAL, John Holden	F/Sgt	27	RAF	03.06.43	FK112
PARKER, Frederick Vincent	W/O	24	RAAF	10.07.43	FK152
PATMAN, James Sydney	F/Sgt	22	RAF	25.04.43	FK371
PHETHEAN, Alfred	Sgt	n/a	RAF	26.08.43	FK373
PHILIPPS, Christopher Posford Martin	F/O	20	RAF	10.07.43	FK152
PINNELL, Walter R.	-	26	*Civil/US*	07.08.42	FK146
PLOSKIN, Ralph Isaac	Sgt	n/a	RAF	16.12.42	FK367
PORTEOUS, Samuel Hart	Sgt	n/a	RAF	20.12.42	FK366
POWER, John Manley	P/O	20	RCAF	19.04.44	FK159
PROUD, Colin Victor	F/Sgt	22	RAF	19.10.43	FK127
QUINNEY, Robert Charles	Sgt	21	RAF	10.05.43	FK376
RANDLE, Gordon Henry	-	?	*Civil/Can*	17.08.42	FK119
RAWLINS, Henry Eric	Sgt	21	RAF [4]	03.06.43	FK112
RAWSON, Douglas Leroy	W/O2	n/a	RCAF	23.11.42	FK122
RAY, Dudley Thomas	F/Sgt	25	RNZAF	03.01.43	FK375
READY, Gordon Leonard	W/O	28	RCAF	15.12.43	FK131
REID, Maurice Cheyne	P/O	25	RAF	01.02.44	FK142
RICE, Daniel Macintyre Mungin	Sgt	30	RAF	10.07.43	FK152
RICE, Walter William	F/Sgt	22	RAF	07.05.44	FK120
ROBINSON, Geoffrey	S/L	n/a	RAF	17.08.42	FK119
ROSS, John	P/O	25	RAF	09.05.44	FK110
RUSSELL, Thomas Geoffrey Notcutt	F/Sgt	21	RAAF	09.05.43	FK155
RYAN, Edward Joseph	F/Sgt	21	RAAF	09.05.44	FK110
SCHRODER, Donald Kilgour	P/O	27	RCAF	19.04.44	FK159
SCOURFIELD, William Haydn	P/O	35	RAF	13.09.44	FK124
SEMPLE, William James	F/Sgt	n/a	RAF	15.02.43	FK150
SIEWART, Henry Morgan	F/L	n/a	RAF	10.03.43	FK154
SIMPKIN, Graham Frederick	Sgt	n/a	RAF	15.12.43	FK131
SIMS, Arthur James	Sgt	n/a	RAF	08.02.44	FK362
SLOGGETT, Douglas William	F/Sgt	n/a	RAF	27.06.43	FK363
SMITH, Arthur Trevor	F/O	32	RAF	07.05.44	FK120
STEWART, Alan Keith	Sgt	20	RAF	21.09.44	FK138
TATLOW, Walter	F/Sgt	39	(CAN)/RAF	10.03.43	FK154
TAYLOR, Cyril Mervyn	F/Sgt	29	RAF	21.09.44	FK138
THOMAS, Stephen George	F/Sgt	21	RAF	15.12.43	FK131
THOMPSON, Jack Irvine	F/Sgt	20	RAAF	15.02.43	FK150
THOMSON, Donald Andrew	W/O2	23	RCAF	28.12.43	FK133
TODD, Philip Matthew	P/O	22	RAF	13.09.44	FK124
TOUPIN, Charles Zotique	W/O1	32	RCAF	28.12.43	FK133
TROVILLO, Frank Leroy	W/O1	24	RCAF	25.04.43	FK371
TRUMAN, Colin Carl	P/O	33	RAAF	15.02.43	FK150

[4] Born in Kenya

TUTTLE, Alan Brian	F/Sgt	20	RAF	28.12.43	FK133
TUXIL, Frank Robert	F/Sgt	n/a	RAF	15.12.43	FK131
VICKERY, Philip Arthur	-	n/a	Civil/Can	22.06.43	FK129
WALKER, Hamilton	Sgt	20	RAF	21.02.43	FK139
WALKINSHAW, Clarnec Victor	Sgt	24	RAF	10.03.43	FK154
WARBURTON, Colin	Sgt	28	RAF	25.04.43	FK371
WATTS, Alan Edwin	Sgt	27	RAF	16.12.42	FK367
WEATHERLEY, Eric Vernon Frederick	F/Sgt	21	RAF	08.07.43	FK141
WESTERN, Arthur	W/O	24	RAF	01.02.44	FK142
WILLIAMS, Albert	Sgt	22	RAF	10.05.43	FK376
WILLIAMS, David Glanmore	P/O	19	RAF	19.10.43	FK127
WILLIAMS, Hugh Garth	Sgt	23	RAF	23.11.42	FK122
WILLIS, Peter McKenzie	F/O	30	RAF	23.11.42	FK122
WOODS, Alfred	F/Sgt	29	RAAF	09.05.44	FK110
WOOTTEN, George Bisgood	Sgt	22	RAAF	10.05.43	FK376
YARWOOD, Basil Herbert	Sgt	n/a	RAF	21.02.43	FK139

Total : 164

RAF : 105 [including one Australian, one Canadian, one South African and one Rhodesian]

RAAF : 25

RCAF : 20

RNZAF : 5

other : 9

A close-up of the first model of tail turret on B-26s and B-26As which mounted a single 0.50-inch machine gun.
(IWM CH17452)

Another close-up of the tail turret with a Flight Sergeant tail gunner installed behind the machine gun. It seems that this was the least comfortable crew position in the aircraft. The 0.50-inch machine gun was a more destructive weapon than the obsolete 0.303 machine guns which still equipped all the RAF multi-engined aircraft in 1942 and in many cases until the end of the war. *(AWM MEC1096)*